MDM

2·24·25

MW01284626

"TV" TOMMY IVO
DRAG RACING'S MASTER SHOWMAN

TOM COTTER
FOREWORD BY DON "THE SNAKE" PRUDHOMME

motorbooks

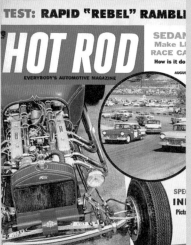

TEST: RAPID "REBEL" RAMBL...

HOT ROD

EVERYBODY'S AUTOMOTIVE MAGAZINE

SEDAN...
Make Li...
RACE CA...
How is it do...

AUGUST...

SPE...
IN...
Pictu...

117-MPH DRAGGIN' TRUCK

CAR CRAFT

18 PAGES — '49 — '51 Ford Customs

AUGUST 1957 25c

Getting Your Car into
MOVIES and TV

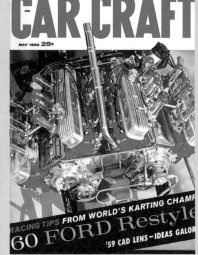

WILL DUAL ENGINE DRAGSTERS TOP 200...

CAR CRAFT

MAY 1960 25c

RACING TIPS FROM WORLD'S KARTING CHAMP...
'60 FORD Restyle...
'59 CAD LENS — IDEAS GALOR...

Competition/Show Stock Tips, How-To, Pictorial

CAR CRAFT

SEPTEMBER 1960 25c

HOW TO —
**BUILD DRAG BODY
FOR 'ALTERED'
COUPE/SEDAN**

KARTING —
**KART CLUTCHES —
NEW DESIGNS FOR
RACING AND FUN**

CUSTOMIZING —
Open Wheel' Caps
SHOWTIME USA
Restyling '60 Pontiac

IVO'S 'RED BOMB'
Look Inside a World's
Drag Record Holder
see page 14

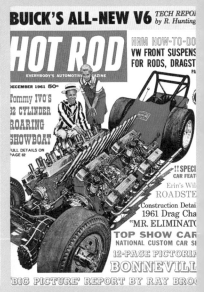

BUICK'S ALL-NEW V6 TECH REPOR...
by R. Hunting...

HOT ROD

EVERYBODY'S AUTOMOTIVE MAGAZINE

DECEMBER 1961 50c

HRM HOW-TO-DO...
VW FRONT SUSPENS...
FOR RODS, DRAGST...
PA...

Tommy IVO'S
32 CYLINDER
ROARING
SHOWBOAT
FULL DETAILS ON
PAGE 62

!! SPECI...
CAR FEAT...
Erin's Wil...
ROADSTE...
Construction Detai...
1961 Drag Cha...
"MR. ELIMINATO..."
TOP SHOW CAR
NATIONAL CUSTOM CAR S...
12-PAGE PICTORIA...
BONNEVILL...
'BIG PICTURE' REPORT BY RAY BRO...

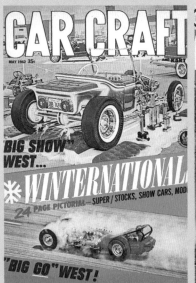

CAR CRAFT

AND KART...

MAY 1962 35c

BIG SHOW"
WEST...
WINTERNATIONAL...
24 PAGE PICTORIAL — SUPER / STOCKS, SHOW CARS, MOD...

"BIG GO" WEST !

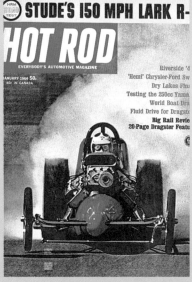

HRM ROAD TEST

STUDE'S 150 MPH LARK R—

HOT ROD

EVERYBODY'S AUTOMOTIVE MAGAZINE

JANUARY 1964 50c
60c IN CANADA

Riverside '...
'Hemi' Chrysler-Ford Sw...
Dry Lakes Fina...
Testing the 250cc Yama...
Two-stage Dra...
World Boat Dra...
Fluid Drive for Dragst...
Big Rail Revie...
20-Page Dragster Featu...

comparing GTOs:'Super' vs Stock!

HIGH PERFORMANCE

YOUR GUIDE TO SPEED

MARCH 1966

Southern
Style...
Racing
-On
Wate...

fact-filled photo salute:
6 Performance Champ...
Two-stage testing the...
Merc 390 'Cyclone...
Ignition from A-Z...

HOT ROD MAGAZINE
COLOR! ACTION! EXCITEMENT!
DRAG RACING
SPECIAL EDITION: an illustrated history

WILD FUNNY CARS!
FUELERS!
PRO STOCKS!
PROFILES:
Don Garlits
Grumpy Jenkins
Dyno Don
TV Tommy Ivo
Mickey Thompson

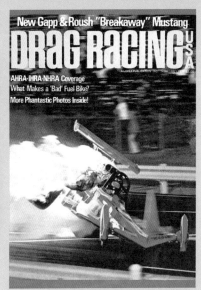

New Gapp & Roush "Breakaway" Mustang
DRAG RACING USA
A LOPEZ PUBLICATION

AHRA·IHRA·NHRA Coverage
What Makes a 'Bad' Fuel Bike?
More Phantastic Photos Inside!

Indy Powerplant X-Ray:
TURBO OFFY-FOYT-CHEVY
HOT ROD
WORLD'S LARGEST AUTOMOTIVE MAGAZINE
COMBINED WITH ROD & CUSTOM

NASCAR: DAYTONA 500
DRAGS: WINTERNATIONAL
OFF-ROAD: SCORE PARKER 400

STREET:
VEGA ENGINE MODS
WHERE IT'S AT IN '75
ENGINE STUDS THAT LIVE
BUTTERA FRAME KITS

TV TOMMY IVO CAPTAINS THE WINNINGEST TEAM IN DRAG RACING, THE NATIONWISE ROD SHOP

Power Tune!
A LOPEZ PUBLICATION MARCH 1979
CAM TIMING TECHNIQUE
SUPER STOCK
& DRAG ILLUSTRATED

SWITCH!!!
BILL "GRUMPY" JENKINS TO NEW CHEVROLET CAMARO

N.E.D. BRACKET FINALS
CHAPTER 12: KING OF THE DRAGSTERS
COLLISION!!!
One of the most hair-raising crash scenes ever filmed!

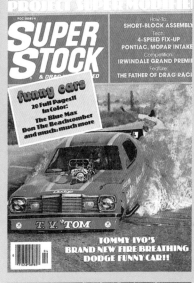

Switch to IHRA
APRIL 1976 · ONE DOLLAR
PROJECT SUPER MODIFIED
SUPER STOCK
& DRAG ILLUSTRATED

How-To:
SHORT-BLOCK ASSEMBLY
Tech:
4-SPEED FIX-UP
PONTIAC, MOPAR INTAKE
Competition:
IRWINDALE GRAND PREMIERE
Feature:
THE FATHER OF DRAG RACING

funny cars
20 Full Pages!!
In Color:
The Blue Max
Don The Beachcomber
and much, much more

TOMMY IVO'S BRAND NEW FIRE BREATHING DODGE FUNNY CAR!!

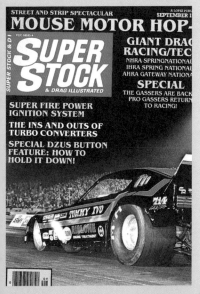

STREET AND STRIP SPECTACULAR
A LOPEZ PUBLICATION SEPTEMBER 1
MOUSE MOTOR HOP-
SUPER STOCK
& DRAG ILLUSTRATED

GIANT DRAG RACING/TECH
NHRA SPRINGNATIONAL
IHRA SPRING NATIONAL
AHRA GATEWAY NATIONAL

SPECIAL
THE GASSERS ARE BACK
PRO GASSERS RETURN TO RACING!

SUPER FIRE POWER IGNITION SYSTEM
THE INS AND OUTS OF TURBO CONVERTERS
SPECIAL DZUS BUTTON FEATURE: HOW TO HOLD IT DOWN!

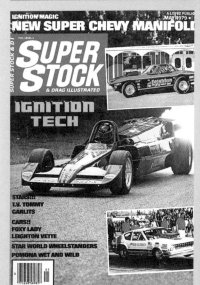

IGNITION MAGIC
A LOPEZ PUBLICATION MAY 1979
NEW SUPER CHEVY MANIFOLD
SUPER STOCK
& DRAG ILLUSTRATED

IGNITION TECH

STARS!!!
T.V. TOMMY
GARLITS
CARS!!
FOXY LADY
LEIGHTON VETTE
STAR WORLD WHEELSTANDERS
POMONA WET AND WILD

This book is dedicated to the six professional heroes of my life:
Dick Bauer, Roger Penske, Humpy Wheeler,
Dr. Olson Huff, Fr. Joseph Kerin, and Chris Economaki. –T. C.

First published in 2011 by Motorbooks, an imprint
of MBI Publishing Company, 400 First Avenue
North, Suite 300, Minneapolis, MN 55401 USA

Copyright © 2011 by Tom Cotter

All rights reserved. With the exception of quoting
brief passages for the purposes of review, no part of
this publication may be reproduced without prior
written permission from the Publisher.

The information in this book is true and complete
to the best of our knowledge. All recommendations
are made without any guarantee on the part of the
author or Publisher, who also disclaims any liability
incurred in connection with the use of this data or
specific details.

We recognize, further, that some words, model
names, and designations mentioned herein are the
property of the trademark holder. We use them for
identification purposes only. This is not an official
publication.

Motorbooks titles are also available at discounts in
bulk quantity for industrial or sales-promotional use.
For details write to Special Sales Manager at
MBI Publishing Company, 400 First Avenue North,
Suite 300, Minneapolis, MN 55401 USA.

To find out more about our books, visit us online at
www.motorbooks.com.

Library of Congress Cataloging-in-Publication Data

Cotter, Tom, 1954–
"TV" Tommy Ivo: drag racing's master showman /
Tom Cotter.
    p. cm.
Includes index.
ISBN 978-0-7603-3892-6 (hb w/ jkt)
1. Ivo, Tommy, 1936- 2. Drag racers–United
States–Biography. 3. Entertainers–United States–
Biography. I. Title.

GV1032.I94C68 2011
796.72092–dc22
[B]
                                    2010039586

Editor: Dennis Pernu
Design manager: Kou Lor
Designer: Chris Fayers
Cover designer: John Barnett/4 Eyes Design

Front cover photo: Bob McClurg
Back cover photo: Paul Sadler

Printed in China

Contents

Foreword By Don "The Snake" Prudhomme

When I was a kid I joined a hot rod club in Burbank called the Road Kings. A young guy named Tommy Ivo had the fastest dragster around, so he was the star of the club. He and I immediately became best friends, and I spent all my spare time in his garage working on his cars. Then I'd go home, get a couple of hours sleep, get up and paint cars in my dad's body shop, then go back to Ivo's to work on his cars all night again. I was young but I loved it.

When he asked if I wanted to hit the road with him and tour the United States, I had my bags packed in a minute. I had no idea where we were going—I had never even been out of California—I just knew that we were going racing. I didn't even care when we were coming home again.

This was the beginning of my career, which lasted 47 years. I give Tommy a lot of credit for helping me become a professional racer. He was a terrific drag racer and businessman, and he taught me that I could actually make a living from racing cars.

Tommy was a hell of a racer; he was as good as they came and was a fierce competitor.

When no one had mag wheels, Ivo had polished Halibrands. When guys were welding up junkyard parts, Ivo had candy apple paint jobs and chrome plating. It was Ivo who helped turn drag racing from a hobby into a profession. He deserves all the credit.

Like lots of friendships, ours turned sour over time when we regularly competed against each other, Tommy in his *Barnstormer* and me in the Greer, Black and Prudhomme car. It became the student racing against the teacher. Plus, I didn't think his practical jokes were as funny as he did. But over time, as we saw each other less, we became friends again.

He was one of those early drag racers who didn't get all the credit he deserved for building the sport to what it is today. That's why I'm glad that this nostalgia movement has given a new life to guys like Ivo. It has given him good reason to come back out to events to see his fans and his fellow racers again.

When I see him at the Hot Rod Reunion at Bakersfield every year, he becomes the same skinny kid with that goofy Howdy Doody grin I met almost 60 years ago.

A young Don Prudhomme checks out his new ride on the set of *Margie*. This was his first professional driving job. Ivo paid the future champion $25 a race to pilot *Showboat*. *Tommy Ivo collection*

Introduction

In 1998, my agency, Cotter Group, was contracted by NASCAR to manage its 50th anniversary celebrations throughout the year. One of the events was called "Hollywood Salutes NASCAR," held at the Wilshire Theatre in Los Angeles. I flew out to L.A. from Charlotte a couple of days early with colleagues Mike Mooney and David Hart.

The night before the event, the three of us went to dinner at a well-known restaurant called The Stinking Rose (a garlic restaurant). During the course of our dinner, David whispered to me, "Look at that guy over there; that's Tommy Ivo." I looked at the gentleman, who was seated at the next table; he was eating dinner with a woman. I said, "That's not Tommy Ivo; he doesn't have blonde hair." But David asked me to keep looking.

As the man and woman were talking, the man smiled at her with that famous huge, toothy grin.

"You're right; it is Ivo," I said.

I couldn't believe it; I had been an Ivo fan since I was a kid growing up on Long Island. My friend Buzzy Brischler and I followed hot rodding and drag racing through the pages of *Hot Rod* magazine from the time we were 10 years old. Ivo was the drag racer with blonde hair and a huge smile, a huge contrast to other drag racers we had seen on those pages. And Ivo was the innovator, first fielding a single-engine car, then one with two engines, then a dragster with four engines! He built a cool T-bucket hot rod with a Buick engine that was like nothing we'd ever seen. His cars were always aesthetically and artistically spot-on.

Even though my interest in drag racing waned as I eventually became interested in sports car racing, I still admired Ivo for his positive image and technical adventures. I had carried one question in particular in my mind for more than 30 years, and now at The Stinking Rose, I had my opportunity to ask.

I waited for a break in the conversation at the next table. My opportunity came when the gentleman, who I believed was Ivo, got up to go to the restroom.

"Excuse me," I said to the woman, "is that Tommy Ivo?"

"Yes, it is," she said. "Oh, please talk to him, because he doesn't think anybody remembers him as a drag racer."

I said I would and returned to my meal.

A few moments later, Ivo returned and sat down. I very politely went to his table and asked, "Are you Tommy Ivo?"

The system of combining each pair of *Showboat*'s engines is apparent —industrial chain couplers were used to tie the rear of one crankshaft to the front of the other engine. *Tommy Ivo collection*

When he displayed that huge grin that seemed to stretch from ear to ear, the answer was obvious.

"Yes, I am," he said.

"I'm glad to meet you," I said as I shook his hand. "Can I ask you a question I've had on my mind since I was a kid?" I asked. He said yes of course.

"How did you hook the four engines together on the *Showboat* dragster and make the four-wheel-drive work?" I asked.

Ivo took out a pen and piece of paper and began detailing the complex drivetrain on the historic drag car.

"We had the two engines on the left facing backwards and the two on the right side facing forward," he said. "So each pair of engines drove its own differential. And we connected each pair of engines together with an industrial chain coupler."

As he continued to diagram, it became obvious to me why this man was so popular with fans: He took the time to meet and greet each fan and to make each one of them feel special—just like he did for me that evening at the Stinking Rose, many decades after his last race.

Little did I realize that just over a decade later I would be lucky enough to chronicle his life and career.

Hopefully I asked Ivo all the right questions during our more than 50 hours of interviews, and all your questions about this man will be answered as well.

Prologue

What Has Four Wheels and Flies?

●Yellow

"TV" Tommy Ivo knew he would be dead in six seconds.

In just six more ticks of the clock, his pain would become extreme, then would be gone as he departed from this world.

It was the 1974 NHRA Winternationals in Pomona, the first event of the season. Ivo was making his fourth qualifying run in a brand-new car. He had made thousands of runs just like it during his career, but this quarter-mile run was different.

In the other lane was John Austin, better known to racers as "Tarzan." Before becoming a driver, Tarzan had been Ivo's crewman for seven seasons, but always quit before season's end. "He'd fire me as his boss, just to prove who was the real boss, even if there was just one week before the end of the season," said Ivo.

So Ivo had an axe to grind. He was damned if he was going to let a former employee beat him in the first race of the season.

The other difference was that this dragster was built by a different chassis builder. Larry Sikora of Cleveland asked Ivo if he could build his new chassis, and Ivo reluctantly agreed. "Woody Gilmore, who had built my other chassis, would turn them out like on a Model T assembly line," Ivo explained. Sikora copied the Gilmore design, but had made a couple of tweaks he felt would give Ivo an advantage. He mounted the rear wing lower and a little farther back on the chassis, feeling it would give the car a "swoopier" look.

In moments, Ivo would realize that was a huge mistake.

●Yellow

Today, teams carefully mix nitromethane fuel according to humidity and barometric pressure using a portable weather station in the pits, but in 1974, according to Ivo, "We'd just lick our finger and hold it up in the air and say, 'Hey, it's getting a little bit cooler.'"

So as they pushed closer to the front of the line, Ivo—nervous about this race against Tarzan—kept leaning out the fuel mixture more and more. "The leaner you make them, the better they run," he said. "If you can get them to run on the aluminum, they go like a son-of-a-gun at the other end. I just didn't want to get beaten by Tarzan, even if it meant I was going to burn a piston as I went by the Christmas tree."

● Yellow

Ivo had done this a thousand times before as he barnstormed his dragsters back and forth across the United States, racing at every little Podunk drag strip for $500, $750, maybe even $1,000 a show. After all, he was the showman, the movie star, the millionaire who drove some of the fastest cars on earth.

Yet, this time was different. His old partner and nemesis Tarzan was in the lane beside him. He couldn't lose.

● Green!

As Ivo mashed the accelerator, he could feel by the seat of his pants that the car was on one hell of a run. It started off without trauma; the Christmas tree turned green and he blasted off ahead of Tarzan. He was relieved to see Tarzan fall back at the start. But because he was driving a rear-engine dragster, Ivo had no idea of the disaster beginning to erupt behind him.

At about 1,200 feet, as he approached the finish line, all hell broke loose. His leaned-out engine erupted in a ferocious ball of fire so fierce that flames enveloped the rear wing, rendering its downward pressure useless. So much for Sikora's swoopy new design.

The next few seconds would be the slowest of Ivo's life.

"Those seconds took ten minutes to happen," he said. "I could give you a detail-by-detail account, it happened that slowly."

Rather than simply burning one piston, all eight pistons welded themselves inside the cylinders, causing the engine block to break and the connecting rods to come out the bottom. A pool of oil spread under the rear tires, which caused the dragster to skate sideways.

Tommy Ivo's crash at the 1974 Winternationals in Pomona, California.
Paul Sadler

"The engine disintegrated like a cheap two-dollar watch," he said.

"As I lifted my foot off the accelerator, I could feel the torque of the motor begin to roll the car over because the lower rear wing couldn't keep the rear end planted. When the car went over, it was sheer terror.

"It wasn't like, 'This is going to hurt.' I was dead; it was over. I knew I wasn't going to walk away this time." He closed his eyes.

Ivo was running at more than 240 miles per hour when his car flipped then rammed into the guardrail rear end first. He had never felt a "thud" so solid, like someone had walloped him in the back with a baseball bat. Video shows a collision so hard that it appeared a small atom bomb had exploded. The engine and drivetrain broke loose from the front of the chassis.

Ivo opened his eyes but thought better when he saw the timing tower was upside down. "This is bad," he thought and slammed them shut again.

With the heavy engine now gone, he was in silent flight, still at more than 200 miles per hour, strapped into the driver's cockpit—a cradle—surrounded by the small roll cage. When he came to the realization that death was imminent, he opened his eyes and decided to enjoy his last few moments on Earth. Suddenly his terror was gone.

"It wasn't pleasant, but it was certainly euphoric," he said. "For a guy who loved experiences, this was my ultimate E-ticket ride. I wouldn't have missed it for the world."

With the engine mass gone, his speed began to slow dramatically. Eventually his E-ticket ride came to a halt, and already NHRA's Safety Safari emergency team was on the scene. As he attempted to exit the wreckage as quickly as possible, he tore his leg on a piece of jagged metal on the dashboard.

He was bleeding, not from the accident, but from his sudden decision to extract himself from the cradle. Otherwise, he didn't have a scratch on him.

He was alive.

As drag racing's master showman, Ivo's first intention was to hop on the safety worker's motorcycle and ride up to the base of the grandstands and take a bow in front of the fans. But he thought better of it because he was wearing Levis instead of the required fireproof safety pants. He didn't want to be further reprimanded by the NHRA.

So he ran back to the pits and immediately called his mother to tell her he was alright; he didn't want his mom to hear from the neighbors that they had just seen on the news that her son got killed. Sara Susanna Ivo had already lost a husband and one son, and Ivo was afraid what might happen if she heard incorrectly that her remaining son had been killed.

Thinking back 35 years after the accident, Ivo's regret was not that he leaned out the fuel mixture on his engine in order to beat Tarzan or that he hadn't worn his fireproof pants; his two regrets were losing to Tarzan and keeping his eyes closed for so long.

"I turned a six-point-zero-two ET going through the lights upside down and backwards," he said. "But Tarzan beat me."

• • •

If you were an American car guy in the 1960s or '70s, you knew Tommy Ivo, if only from the pages of *Hot Rod*. Never before had a drag racer captured the hearts and imaginations of so many fans. In the days when astronauts were walking on the moon, Ivo was building and racing cars that were almost science fiction in their design.

Ivo's clean-cut looks, famous smile, and nonstop enthusiasm for life jumped off the pages and into the minds of young men; he was doing what the rest of us dreamed of.

In the late 1950s, when the foundering sport of competitive drag racing was still being formed, Ivo discovered a diamond in the rough. When dragsters of the day had one engine sitting in front of the driver, Ivo built a dragster with two engines. When other racers caught on to the success of his two-engine concept, Ivo built an outrageous four-engine, four-wheel-drive monster nicknamed the *Showboat*.

When he tired of dragsters, Ivo was one of the early Funny Car pilots. Then he experimented with jet-powered dragsters.

Ivo did it his own way. When others built dragsters from junkyard parts, his were built to the highest standards using glossy "Ivo Red" paint and generous amounts of chrome.

Unlike arch competitors such as Don Garlits and Don Prudhomme, Ivo virtually ignored the National Hot Rod Association's national points championship and instead hauled his cars around the United States, Canada, and even England, receiving appearance money for match racing local favorites and *acting* as the sanctioning body's goodwill ambassador.

Acting. The boyish-looking Ivo left a nearly two-decade career as a successful television and movie star in order to pursue his love of drag racing. It was all about the "show" for Ivo, whether he was performing on stage with Boris Karloff or Roy Rogers, or match racing a different type of costar such as Shirley Muldowney.

Hollywood's loss was drag racing's gain.

Ivo the performer, racer, promoter, engineer, designer, and self-propelled PR-machine experienced all the peaks and valleys that success brings, while never losing that famous "TV" Tommy smile.

Chapter One

The Kid with the Missing Front Teeth

Missing his two front teeth *(opposite)*, seven-year-old Tommy Ivo looked like the authentic American kid that the producers of *Earl Carroll Vanities* were looking for. It opened the door for a two-decade career in show business. *Tommy Ivo collection*

Tommy Ivo didn't grow up in a typical drag racing household. Far from it. He is a first-generation American born to parents who didn't enjoy cars or watching their son risk his life behind the wheel.

Thomas Charles Ivo was born in Denver, Colorado, on April 18, 1936, to Hans Fredrick and Sara Susanna Anna Paulson Ivo. His father was born in Germany, but moved to the United States at the age of one. His mother, who was born in Sweden, boarded a boat to New York all by herself when she was 16 years old, then rode a train to Chicago to live with her sister in 1918.

The Ivos welcomed their first child into the world, a son, in 1929. Donald Paul was born in Chicago and would become Tommy's older brother.

Times were tough during the Depression, and the small family struggled to make ends meet. So when one of Sara's sisters, who lived in Denver, Colorado, suggested the family move there so Hans could take a job as a meat cutter, they packed their bags.

Unable to afford a house, the young family moved into a bungalow on the outskirts of town. Soon, Donald was joined by young Tommy, seven years his junior. "I was a mistake," said Ivo. "With all the complications my mother had giving birth to my brother, she never wanted to get pregnant again. But then there I was!"

With Hans working, Sara cared full-time for her two sons. To help provide for the family, she built a victory garden that was as large as a city block.

Despite being "as poor as church mice," Tommy grew up in the perfect environment. "I lived in Beaver Cleaver's house," he said. "My dad worked, my mom was a housewife, and every night we ate at the dinner table together."

At a young age, it became obvious that young Tommy had a talent for entertaining. The Ivo boys began tap dancing, but according to Tommy, his brother never took to it. "Don had two left feet," he said. Yet he did admit that his older brother had a wild imagination when the two played. "Since he was seven years my senior, he upgraded my imagination to that of a fourteen-year-old. In a way, that tutored me for the make-believe world of movies, which would consume my life for the next twenty years."

The looks are unmistakable. Even at this young age, about two years old, Tommy Ivo had the smile that has made him famous his whole life. *Tommy Ivo collection*

Tommy's first radio broadcast *(opposite)* when he was about six or seven years old in Denver, Colorado. At family gatherings, he would entertain family and friends with all the popular songs of the day. *Tommy Ivo collection*

In 1946, Ivo performed in the stage play *On Borrowed Time* with actor Boris Karloff at the El Patio Theatre in Hollywood. *Tommy Ivo collection*

At family gatherings and over the holidays, four-year-old Tommy would sing popular songs and tap dance for all the adults in the room. Eventually he began performing in local musicals.

Ivo remembers one particularly funny episode as a seven-year-old performer at a Denver stadium production. "I had on my little tux and tails and had to walk down about twenty rows of stairs to get down to the stage," he said. "So I went down there and did my little song and dance. When I finished, I took a bow on stage, then ran back up the stairs. Well, everyone was cheering so much that the man at the top of the stairs said, 'Take another bow.' He meant at the top of the stairs, but I thought he meant back down on the stage. So I ran all the way down and took another bow and then ran back to the top again.

"The audience had by now caught on to what was happening and was going wild, egging me on. So when I got to the top, I ran back down to the stage and took another bow. I wouldn't give up and neither would they. On about my fifth trip, someone up top grabbed me because I probably would have fallen over from exhaustion, running up and down those stairs."

Little did Ivo know that those same show business talents would serve him well decades later as he ran up and down drag strips.

Friends often told Mrs. Ivo, "Oh, you've got to get little Tommy into the movies."

The Denver weather, especially the winters, were not kind to Mrs. Ivo. Even at the young age of 36, her arthritis was so severe she was nearly wheelchair-bound. So in 1943, as an experiment, she and seven-year-old Tommy boarded a bus before the Christmas holidays and traveled west. The journey would hopefully determine two things: whether her arthritis symptoms would be relieved in the warm and dry Los Angeles climate and whether her youngest son had a chance at making it into show business.

Mrs. Ivo, who didn't drive, hauled her young son on buses around L.A. to auditions. At one audition, Tommy was lined up with a dozen other blond-haired, blue-eyed boys. But there was one difference: Ivo had recently lost his baby teeth and had a gaping hole when he smiled. He looked different from the other boys, and his mother was nervous that it was going to be another wasted trip.

Ivo's co-stars in
Earl Carroll Vanities
were Pinky Lee
(left) and Constance
Moore, both big
stars of the day.
Tommy Ivo collection

But Ivo's non–perfect smile made him look authentic, like an all–American kid. He got a key part in *Earl Carroll Vanities*. Tommy's show business career had officially begun.

Additionally, Mrs. Ivo's arthritis symptoms had nearly disappeared during their stay. A phone call back to Denver had Mr. Ivo and Don preparing for the family's move to their new California home.

"It's funny how things work out," Ivo said, "but had it not been that my mother had chronic arthritis, I never would have gotten into the movies. We were poor, and it would have been too expensive for us to go to California and pursue the movies."

Don traveled by himself on a train to L.A., but had to sit on his suitcase because all of the seats were taken up by soldiers. Mr. Ivo packed the family's meager belongings into their Model T Ford sedan and headed west by himself. Near Flagstaff, Arizona, he encountered an ice-covered hill. "He almost didn't make it," said Ivo. "He was back and forth and sideways across the road until he was finally able to bring the car under control."

Apparently Tommy was not the only Ivo with excellent driving skills.

California, Here We Come

Over the next several years, the Ivo clan moved into a series of apartments in the downtown Los Angeles area. Tommy remembers having an icebox in the days before refrigerators, and a man would occasionally deliver large blocks of ice. Less romantically, he remembers hearing rats running through the walls at night.

As young Tommy began to pick up more and more movie deals, the thought of owning a home occurred to his parents, who couldn't afford a house on their own income. The family survived on Mr. Ivo's meat-cutting salary while all of Tommy's acting money was saved in an account under his name.

"My mother asked if I'd like to buy a house for all of us to live in," said Ivo. "So we did." The Ivos moved into a house in Burbank in 1948 and the youngest Ivo became a homeowner at just 12 years old.

Burbank's new junior high school, where Tommy was enrolled, was just five blocks from their new home, an easy walk for the energetic youth.

"Burbank is the Beverly Hills of the San Fernando Valley," said Ivo. "We have our own police and fire departments, and you can go out to walk the dog at two a.m. and think nothing of it. Two miles away in North Hollywood, you'd need a can of mace and an armed guard to attempt that."

Ivo's movie debut was a big, big deal. Backed up by the legendary Woody Herman Orchestra, seven-year-old Tommy stole the show as he danced center stage. *Tommy Ivo collection*

Tommy's father, Hans Ivo, is pictured in his Model T Ford sedan. When the family moved from Denver to Los Angeles in 1943, he packed the car with their meager possessions and drove it to California. *Tommy Ivo collection*

Tommy's brother, Don *(opposite)*, was born seven years before his younger brother. Because of the age difference, they often found it difficult to relate to each other. *Tommy Ivo collection*

Ivo still lives in the same Burbank house he has owned since he was 12, although it has grown from its original 1,000 square feet into a contemporary 4,000-square-foot showplace of his own design.

Soon after moving to Burbank, Ivo's entrepreneurial talents became evident. He constructed an aviary in the backyard where he raised 28-dozen parakeets and sold them to pet stores around town. "I was an industrious little devil," Ivo said. "I was God-given with so much energy that I didn't know what to do with it. I was always building stuff."

By himself, he was an energetic dynamo, but when grouped with contemporaries, he was always the smallest in the crowd. His small stature often caused consternation when teams were being picked during gym class. "I'd always be silently praying, 'Please don't let me be the last one picked. Second to last is OK, but please not last,'" he said.

Ivo believes that cars eventually became his "muscles," and racing became his "varsity team."

Brother Don

The age difference between Tommy and his older brother, Don, was large enough that they never really developed a close relationship. "When he was ten, I was three, and he didn't want a three-year-old hanging around," said Ivo. "It was the same thing when I was ten and he was seventeen."

Despite their age difference, Tommy still idolized his older brother. Tommy said that even though Don had the looks for acting and dancing, he had two left feet, so he joined the service instead. When he died, it left a void in Tommy's life that has never been closed. *Tommy Ivo collection*

Cause & Effect

Tommy Ivo has little doubt that if his brother hadn't been killed in a car accident and had gone on to pursue drag racing as a hobby or occupation, he himself would not have become a drag racer.

"Had he not passed away, most likely I never would have gone drag racing," Ivo said. "After all, he was my big brother, and if he went racing, he would have run the operation, not me. I would have just been his little brother, not the controlling factor.

They began to bond finally when Tommy was 17 and Don was 24 and they began to double-date. Don had just returned from a tour of duty with the U.S. Marines in Korea.

"He had a Model A roadster pickup with a flathead V-8," said Ivo. "He didn't build it, but bought it cheap from someone else. It didn't run well and it didn't have a top, so it rained on the seats."

Don was of slender build—at 5 feet 10 inches, just an inch taller than his younger brother—yet his dream was to become a police officer. His size kept him from joining the force, however, so he became an undercover agent for the Pep Boys auto parts chain. He and another investigator were en route to Ventura, California, in a pickup truck to investigate a shoplifting report when an elderly woman suddenly turned in front of them. Don fell out of the truck's window as it was turning over and, at 24 years old, died instantly.

"We loved each other," said Ivo. "He loved his little brother and I respected my big brother."

The Birds, the Bees, and the Buicks

Tommy Ivo graduated from Burroughs High School in 1954. Prior to graduation, he was fully engaged in being an average student despite his movie and television responsibilities.

While on the movie set, law required that children under 18 act no more than four hours a day, plus have three hours of tutoring with a private teacher and one hour of recreation. By law, Mrs. Ivo was required to be on hand during every scene her son acted until he turned 18.

When he was home, Ivo mostly hung out with Nancy Davidson, who lived across the street. He and Nancy were boyfriend-girlfriend all through junior high school and high school. "In those days, if you had a girlfriend when you graduated from high school, you got married," said Ivo. "The only thing was, I was Presbyterian and Nancy was Roman Catholic, and there was no way her family was going to have anything like that happen. So her father ran me off.

"Her father probably did me the biggest favor anyone has ever done for me in my whole life."

Ivo said that no matter how many movies he made, he always had lots of spare time on his hands. And living in the middle of hot rod heaven, he just had to

have a car when he turned 16. "When I decided to buy a car, Nancy and I hopped on our bicycles and rode to all the new car agencies in town," he said. "We picked up the brochures and spread them all out on the floor in her living room. I asked her which one she liked best. We decided the Buick was pretty sharp-looking."

Ivo went to Burbank Buick to order a Buick Super in bright red, but because of a steel strike in Detroit, the dealer was unable to process the

Tommy went steady with the girl across the street, Nancy Davidson, all through junior high and high school. Here—at ages 17 and 16, respectively— they're pictured together for a high school dance where all the girls presented their dates with a garter to wear on their arm. *Tommy Ivo collection*

Cause & Effect

If Tommy Ivo had married his high school sweetheart, Nancy Davidson, he has no doubts that things would have turned out differently. "We would have gotten married and pumped out a couple of kids," he said. "I probably would have worked in a gas station. No, actually I was too industrious for that; I probably would have continued in the movie business on the production side. But there would have been no way I could have afforded to go racing, at least unless the marriage failed."

Tommy Ivo with his mom, Sara Ivo (left), and his Aunt Becky, who was like a second mother to Tommy. His new 1952 Buick Super is in the background. *Tommy Ivo collection*

order. So while on family vacation in Denver, he called the local dealer just to see if they had a bright red Super. The salesman said, "Yup, we have one right here on the showroom floor."

"I really wanted a Roadmaster, because I wanted four portholes on the front fenders, but because of the extra cost, I had to settle for three portholes," he said. Both the Roadmaster and the Super were built on the large Cadillac-size chassis. "The car had a straight-eight engine with a Dyna-Flush transmission; that's what we called it because you'd step on the gas and wait for it to move. It was sure no hot rod, but I bought it for the looks."

Ivo walked into the Denver dealership and was ignored by the salesmen because even though he was 16 years old, he looked like he was 12. He started honking the horn until a salesmen walked up and asked sarcastically, "What do you think, Son? Would you like to buy it?" Ivo

Practical Jokes

Besides being a great drag racer and the consummate showman, Tommy Ivo was also known among drag racing competitors as a serious practical joker.

For instance, Ivo liked to have fun with Model T spark coils, which could give the unknowing spectator a good dose of voltage without harming them. "I would drive my fifty-two Buick to Bob's Big Boy and park out back," said Ivo. "I'd have wires from the spark coil wired to the car's body, but because of the rubber tires, sitting inside the car, I wouldn't get shocked.

"So when someone would come over to talk to me and lean on the window sill, they would complete the electrical circuit and it would shock the daylights out of them. Or better yet, I'd touch my car's bumper to a buddy's car. When he walked up to put his key in the door, he would get a good shocking."

said yes and whipped out $3,000 in cash and handed it to him. "You could have picked him off the floor when that happened," Ivo said. "I'll bet they treated twelve-year-olds a lot better after that."

Shortly after, Ivo's friend Tom Jandt invited him to the drags. Jandt raced a 1932 Ford three-window coupe with a 410-ci Olds engine. But Ivo had no idea what drag races were. He raced his 1952 Buick at 66.66 miles per hour but wasn't too enthused. "I drove faster than that on the street," he said. "I didn't care about ever going back."

A couple of years later, though, when Ivo started to race his next Buick, a 1955 Century, and then his T-bucket, he did become enthused and Jandt became his helper. "When Tommy became a big-time racer, if he asked me to go to the track with him, it was like being asked by God to go to church," said Jandt.

Chapter Two

Screw the Movies, I'm Going Racing!

If it was the speed that eventually attracted Tommy Ivo to the drag strip, it was the lack of speed that chased him from the movies. "I've done probably a hundred movies and maybe two hundred television shows in my life," said Ivo. "I played the parts of everything from being the proverbial Western Union Telegram delivery man, to being the star lead.

"The movie business was slow, slow, slow, and I did slow, slow, slow for nineteen years."

During those slow years, though, Ivo met and worked with some of the most renowned actors in Hollywood.

"It was all a marvelous experience for a young, adventurous kid," he said. "Once we did a big, big movie called *Plymouth Adventure* about crossing the Atlantic in the Mayflower. It was an all-star cast and included Spencer Tracy, Gene Tierney, and Van Johnson.

"The ship was built on stage with hinges and elevator lifts that would make it go up and down, like it was in a storm. And big electric fans would blow wind and water onto the deck."

Ivo explained that the "inside" of the ship would simulate being hit by a tidal wave and would stand up on its end with bunk beds and cannons rolling across the floor. "When I saw all these stunt men I was wide-eyed," he said.

"In that movie, my character died of tuberculosis, scurvy, and pneumonia, and the make-up people put all kinds of sores on my face. I couldn't wait to get home and walk into my buddies' houses and show their mothers, 'Look at these!' It was great."

It was the balancing act of being a Hollywood kid and a regular neighborhood kid that Ivo credits with his ability to identify with both movie stars and race car mechanics. "Luckily my parents didn't haul me off to Hollywood Professional School, where all the other child actors went to get screwed up," he said. "I just went to a regular school in Burbank. So I really had two lives; my regular childhood kept me grounded and the movies allowed me into a world most people never see."

Oddly enough, the only class Ivo failed in junior high was acting class. "I was supposed to act as the lead in the school play, but I got a movie just before, so obviously I had to take the movie and that left the teacher scrambling," he said.

(Opposite) How many car crazy youths were turned on to Tommy Ivo and his outrageous drag racing cars when the December 1961 issue of *Hot Rod* landed in their mailbox? Unfortunately, the photo shoot brought the seriousness of Ivo's racing endeavors to the attention of TV executives. The car was given the name *Showboat* in this cover story. *Tommy Ivo collection*

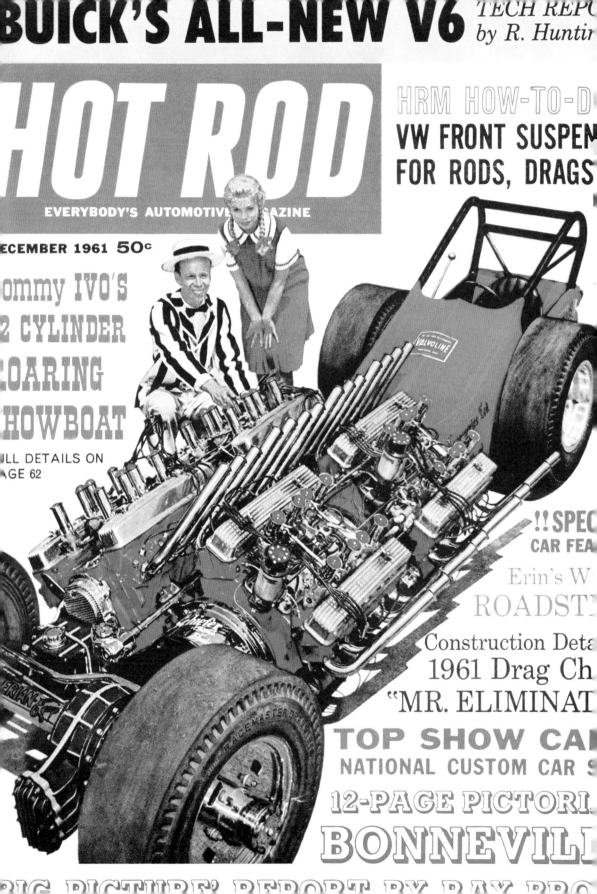

BUICK'S ALL-NEW V6

TECH REPO
by R. Huntin

HOT ROD

EVERYBODY'S AUTOMOTIVE MAGAZINE

ECEMBER 1961 50¢

HRM HOW-TO-D

**VW FRONT SUSPEM
FOR RODS, DRAGS**

ommy IVO'S
2 CYLINDER
OARING
HOWBOAT

LL DETAILS ON
AGE 62

!!SPEC
CAR FEA

Erin's W.
ROADST

Construction Deta
1961 Drag Ch
"MR. ELIMINAT

TOP SHOW CAI
NATIONAL CUSTOM CAR S

12-PAGE PICTORI

BONNEVIL

IG PICTURE' REPORT BY RAY RRO

The second movie Ivo made was called *Song of Arizona*, featuring Roy Rogers and Dale Evans. Here Ivo swears Evans to secrecy. *Tommy Ivo collection*

Also starring in *Song of Arizona* was Gabby Hayes. Ivo was made up to resemble Hayes' character. *Tommy Ivo collection*

Another movie adventure the young Ivo enjoyed was *Bomba, the Jungle Boy*. In the series, Ivo played the friend of Tarzan's son, Bomba. Bomba, played by Johnny Sheffield, taught Ivo that man shouldn't kill animals. The plot twist was that Ivo's dad in the movie was a great white hunter.

"I'd wear my little loincloth and swing through the trees," he said. "The 'vines' we swung on were actually one-and-a-half-inch ropes that were attached to the ceiling. It was a small studio, so they had to move the fake trees around to make it look like different scenes. Once they handed me the wrong rope and I swung right into a tree. Ouch! But can you imagine how much fun all that was?"

Ivo's advantage was that he always looked younger than he was. At 12, he could play an 8-year-old but was better able to understand and follow the directors' needs. Looking young became a real advantage when he was 25 and playing the part of a 17-year-old on the TV series *Margie*. Ivo's mother no longer needed to accompany him to the set, he no longer needed a teacher on site, and he could work more than four hours a day.

"In fact, they would work my ass off working twelve- and fourteen-hour days," he said. "It was nice on my wallet, but hard on the body."

Ivo went on to act in many movies, TV shows, and even Broadway-type theater. As he got older, he appeared on the *Donna Reed Show* and *Leave It to Beaver*, as well as *Margie*. But he could see the end ahead.

In 1955 Ivo acted with comedian Jerry Lewis in *You're Never Too Young.* Ivo remembers Lewis as the goofiest human being he ever met. *Tommy Ivo collection*

Young Tommy Ivo, in the driver's seat of a riding lawn mower but no doubt imagining it is a front-engine dragster. Ivo often played the part of a mischievous boy. In this scene he chased two men across a lawn and into a pool. It's easy to see how these experiences led to a life of practical joking! *Tommy Ivo collection*

"I could tell that I would never grow into a leading man," he said. "I was not going to get Charlton Heston–type parts. I was more the stumbling boyfriend, and the movies I was offered were getting more and more corny. How long could I play that kind of role?"

Being a Hollywood star did give Ivo a leg up on the rest of his drag race competitors. Before he hit the road to race, he created a complete public relations and promotional campaign. He mailed a press kit with head shots and car photos, along with written press releases, to track promoters for distribution to local media prior to his arrival. He would also include a short video clip of him with his dragster.

Ivo's character, Junior *(right)*, played the role of Future Man in the 1948 movie *Song of Idaho*. Tommy Ivo collection

Ivo pilots a fast-moving, horse-drawn stage coach *(far right)* in the film *Song of Idaho*. Tommy Ivo collection

"The promoters would say, 'What do we do with a film clip? The stations out here don't ever air drag racing,'" said Ivo. "I'd tell them to send the clip to their local ABC affiliate and tell them that Haywood Botts, my character from *Margie*, was coming to race his dragster. And the people came out."

Practical Jokes

Lots of practical joking took place on television and movie sets. "Like on the *Margie* set," Ivo said, "we would rehearse a scene where Margie would come to a door, open it, and shout 'Haywood, where are you?'

"Well, between the rehearsal and the actual shoot, we'd sneak over to the door and nail it shut. So with the camera rolling, she would go to grab the door and try to open it. Thinking it was just sticking, she'd really give it a yank. Meanwhile, we're rolling around in laughter off stage. That's how we dealt with the boredom. We were always pulling jokes on each other."

Making Customers for Life

Before *Margie*, Tommy Ivo would work show-to-show. When the TV show or movie he was working on was completed, he was unemployed. This worked out just right in 1960 when he heard from a group of drag strip promoters looking to bring a big-time West Coast racer back East to match race against local heroes. "So I called my movie agent and told him I had a chance to go East and race my dragster all summer," Ivo said. "'Is that OK?' He said to go ahead, so it worked out perfectly for me."

The icing on the cake for these promoters was that since Ivo was a Hollywood star, he could help pack their grandstands with both racing fans and television viewers. "Once these people saw the smoke, fire, and excitement, they became customers for life," Ivo said.

Ivo spent most of a year on the road with his friend and helper Don Prudhomme, match racing from coast-to-coast, border-to-border. That year left a strong impression on the 24-year-old Ivo. "I was chomping at the bit to get back out there the next year," he said after his first touring season. "With my movie and television credentials, it gave drag racing tracks a big shot in the arm when we toured that year."

Ivo appears in character as Haywood Botts with *Margie* co-star Cynthia Pepper in his last major acting role.
Tommy Ivo collection

The problem was, by 1961 Ivo had a regular "gig" playing 17-year-old Haywood Botts in the successful *Margie* TV series. Ivo said the show's executives and producers probably knew he was involved in drag racing, but they didn't seem to mind, imagining that racing his Cadillac at a local track was better than racing it in the streets. That all changed, though, with a photo shoot for the December 1961 issue of *Hot Rod* magazine.

Hot Rod planned to feature Ivo's four-motor *Showboat* dragster on the cover, and photo editor Eric Rickman said to Ivo, "Listen, let's shoot the photo of the car on the *Margie* set."

"Things were pretty loosey-goosey half a century ago, so we didn't ask for any special permission," Ivo said.

Ivo towed his impressive dragster onto the TV set and unloaded it. He posed next to his dragster in his Haywood Botts outfit—straw hat, striped jacket—with his *Margie* co-star, Cynthia Pepper, next to him. It is one of the most memorable *Hot Rod* covers ever (see page 33).

"Is that the car you race?" asked some studio executives who had wandered out.

"Yeah," Ivo responded, continuing with the shoot.

"And at that moment, I could hear office doors slam all the way on the other end of the set," Ivo said. "Afraid for the health and safety of one of their stars, I was presented with an addendum to my contract that

Ivo behind the wheel of the *Margie* show's Stutz Bearcat replica. When *Margie* was cancelled, Ivo could finally drive a much faster car without fear of losing his acting contract.
Tommy Ivo collection

forbade me from racing. Period. And money talks, so I had to sign it. I was making eight hundred dollars a week. I knew what side my bread was buttered on."

He was also making money in drag racing, about $500 a week, but that was before expenses, including motels, Prudhomme's wages, fuel, and meals. He was certainly making more money from his acting job.

If he hadn't signed the new contract, the producers would have written his character—and him—out of the show, Ivo said.

So Ivo developed Plan B, initially hiring Prudhomme, then Ron Pellegrini and later Tom McCourry, to drive *Showboat* on a tour around the United States. It would still be Tommy Ivo's car, he just wouldn't drive it.

A young Don Prudhomme worked during the day at his father's body shop, but on evenings and weekends he helped Ivo work on his race cars. Here he paints a body panel for Ivo's four-motor car. *Tommy Ivo collection*

The arrangement worked well for the year, but then, because of a television time slot and sponsor change, *Margie* was cancelled in late summer of 1962. The cast, writers, directors, and producers were all depressed when they heard the news.

And Ivo? He went into his dressing room, shut the door, and shouted, "'Hooray!' I'm sure everyone else heard me jumping around and doing cartwheels in there, because now I could go drag racing full-time!

"I had played the part of an orphan, had gone diving for treasure, and fought it out with Gene Autry and Roy Rogers. The movies were still bitchin', and I liked doing them, but I had done it for nineteen years. Drag racing was my new love."

Instead of hitting the road in the *Showboat*, which had suddenly become outdated when the NHRA started allowing competitors to run on nitromethane, Ivo put the wheels in motion to build his next touring car, *Barnstormer*.

Ivo took one more role, a very small part as a telegram delivery man on the TV show *Please Don't Eat the Daisies*, but after he delivered his few lines, he put the money into his pocket and never looked back.

Road Kings Car Club

If Tommy Ivo had grown up in the Bronx, perhaps he would have gotten involved in baseball. But growing up in Southern California made it much easier to fall into the area's intense car culture. Burbank was home to what was probably America's first drag racing club, the Road Kings, founded in November 1952 by 18-year-old Jim Miles and a couple of his friends.

Meetings were every Sunday night and dues were 25 cents per week. Seventeen people attended the first meeting. "I had just graduated high school and raced my nineteen forty-nine Ford," said Miles, the only charter member still active in the club. "Ivo joined when he was driving his brand-new nineteen fifty-five Buick. He had just graduated high school in nineteen fifty-four.

"When the club was organized, we mostly raced at Saugus, but then in nineteen fifty-five, when San Fernando opened, we mostly ran there, then at Colton and Santa Ana too."

Miles went on to race several cars, mostly Fords, but ultimately raced a Fuel Altered Fiat coupe until 1977.

Eventually Ivo became the star of the club because he built the best-looking cars, such as his T-bucket and the twin-engine car, and was winning races.

Another child actor and hot rodder, Skip Torgerson, also became a Road Kings member. "I met Tommy in nineteen fifty-five or fifty-six," said Torgerson. "I was also a young actor and met Tommy on the set of a movie called *A Boy with a Knife*. We also acted together in *Blackboard Jungle*. Ivo mentioned to me that he was building a roadster, and I said, 'So am I!' Not too long afterwards he finished his roadster and came

Practical Jokes

Don Prudhomme was often on the wrong side of Ivo's jokes. "He was not mean, but after a while, the jokes would just wear on me," said Prudhomme. "He was like a kid in a man's body.

"One time he was over at my house and helping me work on the dragster. I had a set of headers hanging on the wall and we were getting ready to mount them, but I walked into the house for a few minutes. While I was away, Ivo painted the backside of the headers with wet paint, so when I grabbed them, I got paint all over my fingers."

Don Prudhomme waves "hello" to his old friend Tommy. *Tommy Ivo collection*

driving it into Bob's Big Boy drive-in. He invited me to join the Road Kings car club and we've been friends ever since."

Torgerson was able to get his friend Don Prudhomme invited to join as well, but his initiation was brutal. Prudhomme had to crawl into Bob's Big Boy wearing nothing but a diaper and ask the waitress for milk for the baby bottle that was tied around his neck. Not surprisingly, Ivo was in charge of initiations.

"I hung around Ivo's house and helped him work on his cars," said Torgerson. "But mostly Ivo did everything himself and everyone stood around watching. After we all left, he'd stay up all night and work, then sleep all day. He keeps those same crazy hours today."

Ivo neighbor and friend Ed Janke joined the Road Kings in 1957. "Since I was ten years old, I've been drag racing crazy," said Janke, who eventually drove dragsters himself. "My mom or dad would drop me off either at the Santa Ana or Saugus tracks on the weekend.

"I started to go to the track with Ivo and I remember one time we had raced at Fremont up near San Francisco. We left the track and had come over the mountains and were coming back toward L.A. We stopped at a gas station to clean up and Ivo said, 'I left my hundred-and-fifty-mile-per-hour watch in the men's room at the track. We need to go back.' Tommy had won this watch for being the first guy to go a hundred and fifty miles per hour at San Gabriel. So we drove all the way back to the track, but the watch wasn't there.

"Recently I told Tommy to keep his eyes open on eBay; that it will probably show up there eventually."

Janke has two lasting impressions of Ivo's early drag racing days. "I once drove his two-engine car, and I have no idea how his skinny little legs had the strength to push that clutch down. And he ran that blown fuel dragster all those years out of the back of a Cadillac. We'd all say, 'How does he do that?'"

Miles said that his club went dormant in 1964 when racers were too busy to attend the mandatory Sunday-night meetings (other Road King members who either built or drove drag cars nationally were Prudhomme, Tom McCourry, Rod Peppmuller, Kenny Safford, and Bob Muravez). Then in 1987, the club was reactivated, mostly as a hot rod club. Today there are one hundred members.

"But back in the early nineteen sixties, when we only had twenty-seven members, two of them—Ivo and Prudhomme—became touring professionals," said Miles. "We were proud of that."

Practical Jokes

Veteran drag racer Tom McEwen remembers one night at a motel near the Fremont Dragway in Northern California. The hotel sat behind a gas station that had waste oil stored in 55-gallon drums. "Prudhomme and [Tom] McCourry got a five-gallon bucket of this oil and a couple of old feather pillows," said McEwen. "It's about three a.m. and they kicked Ivo's hotel door open. When he sat up in bed, they threw the bucket of oil on him then coated him with feathers. The guy who owned the hotel was going to put them in jail. They had to pay for the damages."

Chapter Three

Life as a California Drag Racer

Even as a full-time drag racer, Ivo still acted as if he were in a theatrical production. His smiling face graced the covers of car magazines across the United States, but his pretty-boy image did not match reality.

"I played the part of a rich, millionaire playboy movie star who just happened to drag race," said Ivo. "But the public never saw me rolling around in the muck, the mud, and the dirt when I was putting cars together."

Being a photogenic grease monkey, though, was exactly what was necessary during this transitional time in drag racing. Drag racing historian and author Tom Madigan said that Ivo was in exactly the right place at the right time. "He developed into the consummate, professional California drag racing guy," said Madigan. "He was living and racing during a critical turning point for the sport.

"Ivo had an image and people flocked to him in the pits. He raced with a custom black leather jacket with *Poison Ivo* embroidered on the back, black leather pants, red goggles, a Tony Nancy fireproof facemask. He was one of *the* guys responsible for the transition of the sport from the homemade dragster built by a gas station attendant to the professional driver with state-of-the-art equipment."

As a racer, Ivo matured during a time when Top Fuel cars were king, from 1962 to 1968. Funny Cars had not yet arrived on the scene, so fans flocked to drag strips across the country to see the rails. Ninety dragsters would show up at Bakersfield for 32 positions. Every car owner wanted their cars to have beautiful bodywork and brilliant paint jobs in addition to being fast. Cars were reaching 210 to 215 miles per hour, and because builders were still naïve, aerodynamics were minimal.

Cars were darting, blowers were exploding, and clutches were cutting dragsters in half.

"Drivers were all braver than Dick Tracy," said Madigan. "The cars were getting longer and longer, but if drivers tried something new, it often blew back in their faces. The price was that you lost a guy once in a while."

The speeds climbed to 220, 240 miles per hour.

California was the hub for the Top Fuel hysteria reported in the pages of hot rod and drag racing magazines to teens in places like Long Island. Once in a while, ambassadors like Ivo brought that excitement to the

Getting paid to run IHRA events (opposite), Ivo didn't have to rely on match races in between IHRA qualifying and racing to stay in business. Tommy Ivo collection

How Rich Was Ivo?

Millionaire. Playboy. Actor. Drag racer. Ivo wore all these hats at the same time. And even though he never dispelled any of those titles, his bankbook was never as flush as the public imagined. Ivo used the myths of his wealth to get appearance opportunities at tracks because those myths attracted fans. Like any actor, he was playing a character.

"I wouldn't call him a California rich kid," said Don Prudhomme. "But he had a little bit of money when nobody else had any. He spent it wisely and had nice cars."

"Everyone thought I was shot in the ass with diamonds," said Ivo. "But what they didn't know was that I didn't go out and buy everything, I built it myself."

When Ivo was acting, he'd make $150 to $200 a day and $500 to $700 a week, the going rate for actors in the 1950s. "The most money I ever made was during the *Margie* series, when I earned eight hundred dollars a week," he said. Ivo actually earned more from racing, which was still modest.

He is most proud of the Burbank house he bought for $12,000 when he was 12 years old. Today the magnificent home has quadrupled in size and is valued in the seven figures.

Now that was a good investment.

masses in places like Concord, North Carolina; Islip, New York; and Saskatoon, Saskatchewan.

"I don't think any driver has ever driven as many races as I have," said Ivo. "I ran at least seventy races a year and as many as one hundred."

"[Ivo] was tough, and he figured out early on that he could make more money as a showman than as a serious competitor," said 17-time national champion Don "Big Daddy" Garlits. "In those days, competitive drag racing didn't pay very much. He wasn't rich like everyone thought he was. So he had to make money."

"Making money" was a phrase not often used around drag racing in those days. "If we got a fifty-dollar savings bond or a case of oil, we thought the world came to an end," said Madigan, who also raced Top Fuel cars during the era. "And if you won five gallons of nitro, how could you ask for anything more?

"But Ivo changed the game. He would make three runs and get a thousand dollars. He took his theatrical training and brought it to the track; he was the showman."

One young Californian who always kept his eyes on Ivo was none other than John Force. Force, the winningest Funny Car driver in history with 15 championships, was an impressionable youth who traveled to Southern California drag strips with his uncle. "He was a talented kid who loved hot rods, just like me and Dale Earnhardt," said Force. "He was a guy I learned a lot from as a kid, because he was an entertainer."

Force believes that Ivo had some influence on his own entertaining style because both could keep people laughing even if they didn't win. "He brought showmanship to drag racing," said Force. "He'd come to a drag race with a two-engine dragster, and when others copied him, he'd build one with four engines! Have you ever seen that monstrosity?"

Force credits Ivo with entertaining drag racing fans, a role he assumes today. "We're P. T. Barnum. We're on stage. Ivo taught me to make people laugh even when I wasn't winning. He taught me to look fans in the eye when I signed autographs, to ask their name and to make them feel special."

Another young enthusiast who was entertained by Ivo was Greg Sharp. A former police officer, Sharp is now curator at the Wally Parks NHRA Motorsports Museum in Pomona, California. "I took

Inez Ivo was a fixture at the race tracks, and often guided Tommy back to the starting line after a burnout. Problem was Tommy couldn't figure out what she was trying to signal to him. *Tommy Ivo collection*

a picture when I was fourteen years old of a nineteen thirty-four Chevy coupe that I liked at Lions Drag Strip, and in the background is a big crowd of people," said Sharp. "They were all looking at Tommy Ivo's twin-engine dragster.

"We'd kid him about being 'Cecil B. d'Ivo.' He was all about showmanship, quality of equipment, and style. He always did things first class. And he had two high-profile and glamorous careers. Most people never have even one of those careers, but instead spend their days putting together widgets."

Sharp said that Ivo broke the mold because he was a crowd favorite even though he never won an NHRA national event. "He was runner-up a couple of times, but because he needed to make money, he always left after the first day of qualifying to match race at several other tracks, then return for final eliminations. He'd drive to drag strips towing his dragster with a new Cadillac. He was a movie star who drove dragsters at a hundred and eighty miles per hour. Ivo was always a big spectator draw.

"He was the first drag racer who gave away pictures of his cars and signed autographs for fans, which was popular in NASCAR, but totally unheard of in drag racing at the time. He made a lot of money for promoters."

Inez Anderson and Tommy went on a lengthy "date" during an opening in the drag racing schedule and visited Europe and Egypt. *Tommy Ivo collection*

Mr. Goody Two Shoes

Ivo wore clean white T-shirts, kept his blonde hair groomed and combed, and was never publicly involved in scandals. He was the kind of drag racer your mother would invite over for dinner. "I was a teetotaler," he said. "I had never even tried a cigarette or alcohol."

But one day his curiosity got the best of him. He was racing his *Barnstormer* dragster with pal Dave Zeuschel, who liked to drink Singapore slings. "He'd get pretty brave when he started drinking those things," Ivo said. "So one night we're at the bar and I said, 'Let me taste that.' To me it tasted like soda pop, so I drank the rest of it. So Zeuschel orders two more.

"I was showing off, so I drank those as well. Then I said, 'Bartender, two more.' I drank five of those suckers, and as I was sliding under the table, I remember asking for someone to remember to get the receipt."

That night Ivo's friends drove him home, propped him up next to the front door of his house, and rang the doorbell. "I didn't feel good for a week," he said. "That drinking thing is no good for you."

No Nationals

Until 1965, only two NHRA national events existed: the Winternationals in Pomona and the U.S. Nationals in Indianapolis. Drag racing was still considered a hobby sport at the time because it cost money to participate, but produced no money, even for wins or records.

Most drag racers would go to one drag strip, week in and week out. Sharp believes that by 1965, Ivo was already established as a touring match racer and would have had difficulty changing formats. "Promoters were already signing him up for appearances a year ahead of time," said Sharp. "He gave up winning championships and breaking records for money, of which he earned a lot before anyone else."

One of Sharp's colleagues at the NHRA Museum is executive director Tony Thacker. Thacker, who grew up in England as a hot rod–crazy youth, read about Ivo while delivering newspapers. "I'd always read about Ivo in *Hot Rod* magazine," he said. "Tommy always had the brightest-colored cars and raced under the bluest skies. Not like we had in England. After my father took me to see some drag races as a kid, I was hooked. I finally moved to California when I was thirty-eight years old."

A Normal Life, Temporarily

Ivo went to Indy to race in 1970 and met Inez Anderson, his crewman John "Tarzan" Austin's girlfriend. Inez worked for Gentleman Joe Schubeck, who manufactured drag racing parts and later drove the four-wheel-drive *Hurst Hairy Olds* Toronado.

"Inez was smitten with Tarzan and came to the next race in New Orleans to be with him," said Ivo. "And Tarzan says to me, 'Ahhh, here comes that dizzy dame again,' and gives her the brush-off. So, since he shunned her, I kept her entertained for the weekend, and that's how we met."

Inez and Ivo began dating and traveled to races together on and off for almost two years. Once, when he was racing in the East and the next race weekend was rained out, Ivo popped the question. No, not that question.

"Have you ever been to Europe?" he asked. When she said no, they took a quick detour to Washington, D.C., and got her an emergency passport by telling the official that her dad was dying in Europe. "The guy behind the desk said, 'Yeah, you'd be surprised how many people are dying in Europe during tourist season.'"

They began their travels in England then continued through France and Italy, which is where he saw a poster in the window of a travel agency. It showed the great pyramids in Egypt.

"I thought, 'Oh, man, I'd like to go there,'" he said. "So after just a few days in Europe, we were off to Egypt, which is my favorite place in the world. Being of Christian descent, I'd always thought of

IHRA vs NHRA

Many of Ivo's competitors mention that even though Ivo was the consummate touring professional, he never won an NHRA National event. This is true, even though Ivo did make it into the finals many times.

In the 1950s through 1970s, the National Hot Rod Association wasn't the only game in town. Other players included the International Hot Rod Association (IHRA) and the American Hot Rod Association (AHRA). Even NASCAR sanctioned some drag races.

Drag racing was still a free-for-all sport, with several governing bodies all vying for a position of domination. Ivo wasn't loyal to any particular sanctioning body and ran events with all of them, as well as some of the outlaw groups.

"The IHRA was just about as strong as the NHRA at the time," said Ivo. "I was guaranteed money to race in three IHRA events, won two of them, and finished runner-up in the third. It was the same thing when I won the NASCAR Summer Nationals in 1960. I found it was helpful to stay at the track all weekend."

Ultimately the NHRA became the dominant player, but Ivo has no regrets: "I did win a few of national events, just with other sanctioning bodies."

Tommy and Inez tied the knot in 1972. The couple took a two-and-a-half-month honeymoon around the world. Eventually the bliss wore off as Ivo spent time on the road and Inez yearned for a quiet home life. *Tommy Ivo collection*

Christ as way back toward the beginning of time. But here I was, standing inside pyramids that were twice as old as Christ."

The hook was set. Ivo and Inez were officially an item. "I mean, I took a date to Europe and Egypt," he said.

On the flight home, Inez was practicing her signature. "She had very fancy handwriting," said Ivo. "And she was practicing pairing the double I's in Inez and Ivo. I knew I was in trouble then."

Meeting Inez was a life-changing event for Ivo. At about this time, he was becoming bored with life on the road. The couple had a California wedding in 1972 and went on a two-and-a-half-month worldwide honeymoon, or, as Ivo called it, "lollygagging around the world." The couple stayed at the Hotel Continental overlooking the Taj Mahal, visited Russia when it was too cold for comfort, and spent time in Bombay, Bangkok, Hong Kong, and Tokyo. Ivo purchased artworks from many of these countries, and they adorn his house today.

The Ivos bought a second home in Cleveland, which functioned as the base for his East Coast racing operations. "It became hard to work out in the cold garage twenty-four hours a day when I had a happy new bride waiting in the house for me," he said.

At first, Inez enjoyed the travel. "She would help guide me when I was backing up my Funny Car," he said. "She wore those knee-high white boots and miniskirts, which were fashionable at the time, and she'd be with me in front of all those fans. But I never could figure out which way she was guiding me! She became somewhat of a celebrity herself and signed autographs."

But according to Ivo, it was never a real marriage. "Life on the road was a bitch and living out of a suitcase was impossible for Inez," said Ivo. "She was a high-maintenance piece."

Eventually she yearned for a real home life. Ironically, the exciting travel that began their relationship also ended it. The Ivos divorced in 1978. "It wasn't because we were fighting all the time," he said, "it just didn't work. We were still best friends."

In fact, a couple of years later she moved back in with him in California for almost four more years and even helped Ivo celebrate his 50th birthday in China. "I almost said, 'I do,' again," he said. "But it's a good thing I didn't. Because it seems as though you just can't put toothpaste back in the tube. We both went our separate ways once again, but still remain good friends."

Vampire-Like Sleeping Habits

Tommy Ivo runs on Ivo Time, which is very different than any other time zone. He said even though it drives him crazy, his body doesn't run on a regular 24-hour clock. "I'm just so hyper I don't fall asleep until the sun comes," he explained.

(Author note: This is true. While writing this book, I would arrive at Ivo's house in the early

Even though Tommy and Inez were divorced, they remained good friends and moved back together again for almost four years. This photo was taken in China when Tommy and Inez celebrated his fiftieth birthday together. *Tommy Ivo collection*

Practical Jokes

One night, Tom McCourry, Bob Muravez, and I were sitting in Bob's Big Boy, bored to death. Skip Torgerson had told me he was going to bed early that night, so we decided to go over to his house and give him some grief.

I was the mad bomber of Burbank, you understand—no one I knew was safe. We were all out of M-80s, our favorite explosive for this type of attack, but Kent Fuller had just shown me how to make a bomb by filling a small balloon with oxygen and acetylene and putting it in a paper bag that you then lit on fire. The bomb Fuller showed me didn't make much noise, so we went down to the all-night drug store and got a *big* balloon. Unfortunately, Fuller had neglected to tell me not to make it too big,

because it was a gas explosion with a lot of concussion.

So, off to Skip's we went, all laughing—and McCourry smoking, no less. If we had set that balloon off in the car, it would've blown out all the windows and rung our bells pretty good. We slipped the balloon under Skip's bedroom window, between his house and his neighbor's, and laid it on a long rolled-up strip of newspaper that we lit as a fuse. We ran halfway down the block and stood there with our hands cupped over our ears. Well, it still wasn't very loud, but the concussion shook the ground under our feet and blew all the windows out of Skip's house as well as his neighbor's. I stuck to M-80s only from then on!

afternoon, about the time Tommy was waking up. Our interviews would go well for five or six hours, but then I'd start getting tired around suppertime. Ivo, however, was raring to go on for another few hours. Somehow, we both compromised and got the job done.)

Ivo's altered sleeping cycle is also partly a result of drag racing and his intense touring schedule. "I'd race every Saturday and Sunday," he said. "I'd get up at one o'clock in the afternoon Saturday and race into the evening. Then I'd drive all night long to the next track three hundred or four hundred miles away.

"Most of the other guys needed 'bennies' [Benzedrine] or some other kind of stimulant," he explained, "but I was too well rested from getting up late to fall asleep. A couple of bottles of Coke would do the trick for me."

When Ivo was traveling and needed to repair his car on the road, he would often use garages of friendly competitors or enthusiasts. In the Washington, D.C., area, he used a Ferrari dealership to work on his dragster in the evening. "When the mechanics at the dealership quit for the day, I'd go in and work like an elf all night long," he said. "Then when they came in and said 'Good morning' at eight a.m., I'd say good night. After getting into this habit for so many years of racing on the road, it permanently altered my sleep patterns."

Who Do You Think You Are, Tommy Ivo?

One night when Ivo was racing at a small drag strip in Piedmont, North Carolina, his crewman Tarzan decided to go out drinking. "I was brought up as pure as the driven snow: no smoking and no drinking," said Ivo. "So I decided to go see a movie instead."

There was only one theater in the area, in nearby Winston-Salem. So Ivo drove there and watched a double feature. Afterward, Ivo, as he puts it, was "hauling the mail" back to his hotel. "A cop pulled me over for speeding," he said. "There was nobody on the road except for him and me. So he gave me the ticket and drove off. I ripped it up and threw it into the air and never thought about it again."

But two years later, a clerk for the county hadn't forgotten Thomas Ivo quite as easily. "Some bookworm clerk way down in the bottom of city hall saw the local newspaper announcing that Tommy Ivo is coming back to town to race again," said Ivo. "So he dug back into the archives and came up with the record of my unpaid ticket. So it's six a.m. and I'm sleeping in my hotel room when I get a bang-bang-bang on the door."

"Are you Thomas Ivo?" asked the police officer.

"Yes I am," said Ivo.

"Well please put your clothes on, you're going to jail," said the police officer.

"And off to jail they took me," said Ivo, who was charged $25 for his speeding ticket and the additional penalties. The local papers picked it up and it made front-page news. The headline read "Not Fast Enough."

"The crowd was so good on race day that the promoter gave me back my $25 and said, 'I couldn't buy that type of publicity.'"

Ivo and Don Garlits (right) have always had a respectful relationship. They have match raced each other numerous times at small tracks across the United States, and both have high praise for each other's driving styles. This photo was taken at Atco Dragway in New Jersey in 1967. *Tommy Ivo collection*

Anyone who ever traveled with Ivo can attest to that. "Ivo was like a vampire," said Don Garlits. "He couldn't sleep at night and because he was so blonde, he couldn't be out in the sun during the day. . . . Even today he likes to call me in the middle of the night."

Don Prudhomme spent a solid year traveling with Ivo when he fielded the twin-motor dragster. "Even when he was home, I'd go over there after work and he'd still be in his pajamas," said Prudhomme. "But when we were on the road, he traveled with these black-out curtains because the room had to be pitch-black, even when the sun was out."

Chapter Four

Touring the U. S., ¼ Mile at a Time

Ivo had the all-American, clean-cut looks of an athlete or a movie star *(opposite)*, which was exactly the image that drag racing needed at the time. *Tommy Ivo collection*

Tommy Ivo may have owned a home in Burbank, California, but he lived in North America: from sea to shining sea, from the Mexican border and into Canada.

Ivo took a different path in drag racing than did his contemporaries. Instead of staying close to his California home base, which was the hot rod and drag racing center of the universe, he became drag racing's ambassador and took his show on the road. For 22 years, Ivo toured with various drag cars, racing for any drag strip promoter who could afford his $500, $750, or eventually $1,500 appearance fees.

He spent most of his time in the East, where "California drag racers" were a breed that enthusiasts read about in magazines. When Ivo came to town, it was a fan's chance to see a real California drag racer up close. Ivo brought a fresh, clean image of West Coast drag racing to the East that did much to spread the gospel of drag racing to the speed-hungry masses.

Since most of the match racing took place in the eastern part of the Midwest and up and down the East Coast, Ivo often worked at a disadvantage to most other racers, who had shops closer than 3,000 miles away. If Don Garlits needed to move his engine back by 2 inches, he could easily transport his car back home to Florida to perform the modification before the following weekend. Ivo, on the other hand, worked a lot of weekdays between races to promote the next race and often had to live with a pending modification until he had a break in his schedule.

Another difference was that a racer like Garlits owned a speed shop back home and didn't need drag racing to pay his mortgage. Ivo, on the other hand, was probably the first driver who made his living strictly from racing.

Ivo started his touring career on the belief that fans would pay to see the California actor/hot rodder race his exotic two-engine dragster. Initially he charged promoters $500 a stop (real money in 1960), left his Burbank home in March, and didn't return until November.

The rumor mill churned out news that Ivo was the millionaire racer who made all his money from acting, but that was far from the truth. Ivo, however, never tried to dispel those rumors, which added to his persona. He sent out TV clips of himself to stations in racing markets, drove up

One thing Ivo loved most about touring the country with his dragster was being a tourist. Here he stands at a monument for the Painted Canyon in North Dakota in 1963, while Ivo's crewman and friend Tom McCourry climbs on a sign there. *Tommy Ivo collection*

in a fancy Cadillac with California license plates, and pulled an exotic race car on a trailer. Fans flocked to see him. With any luck—or so the promoters hoped—those fans would get turned on to drag racing and return the next week when Ivo was onto the next town.

And it all started with his friend, Don Prudhomme.

Touring with the Twin

To Prudhomme, Ivo was an old man. But then, all 19-year-olds look at 24-year-olds as old men. The two hit the road in March 1960 and began an adventure that has lasted most of both of their lifetimes.

"It was the best time of my life," said Ivo. "We drove seventy thousand miles that year, all on two-lane roads. I watched the interstate system grow up. . . . It was scary to drive down the ice-covered roads of Loveland Pass in the Rockies with burned-out brakes in a four-thousand-pound Cadillac towing a trailer."

When Ivo met Prudhomme, he was just a kid putting together a hot rod. "When I was introduced to Don, he wanted to talk to me because he was putting a Buick engine in his roadster," Ivo said. "He was a pretty good painter, so I told him I'd help him with his roadster if he painted my dragster."

Prudhomme remembers the conversation. "Ivo said to me, 'Hey, I'm going on this tour. Want to come?'" said Prudhomme. "I'd never even

Practical Jokes

When he was touring with the young Don Prudhomme in 1960, Ivo would replace the shampoo in the hotel shower with motor oil just before Prudhomme went into the bathroom. The more water he added to his hair, the more the oily solution resembled axle grease. The result would be an angry Prudhomme who had to deal with the massive oil slick on his head.

Ivo believes his practical joking may have a couple origins.

Ivo's father, Hans, was also a joker. "He was a real character," said Ivo. "During the holidays, he'd gather all the children around in a circle and play the game 'Pinch Me, Don't Smile.'" Mr. Ivo would pick one child and pinch his nose. Then each kid would in turn pinch the nose of the kid next to him or her. Unknown to that first child though, but obvious to everyone else, was that Hans' fingers were coated with black chimney soot and the child's nose was black.

According to Ivo, another possible reason for his lifelong obsession with jokes was that in the movies, he often played the part of a younger kid who played jokes on everybody else. Also, "Movie sets are generally a very lighthearted atmosphere, where lots of joking goes on," he added.

been out of California. He was actually the first guy I had ever met who could just pack his bags and just go. I had no idea where we were going, but I knew we were going racing."

So Prudhomme took the engine out of his roadster, strapped it to Ivo's trailer as a spare, and said goodbye to his parents. They headed first to Denver, where they dropped off Ivo's mother at her sister's house. "My mom hitched a free ride with us to Denver," said Ivo. "Our first scheduled tour appearance was at Continental Divide Raceway. She hadn't seen her sister in years, so this was too good a chance to pass up."

Then they kept driving. "I have a picture of him behind the wheel of his Cadillac with his big Howdy Doody smile," said Prudhomme. "He was quite a character, just a skin-and-bones kind of guy. He was different than

Ivo and Prudhomme get ready to hit the road for a match racing safari in 1960. The pair drove 70,000 miles that year, nearly all on two-lane roads. They left with their Cadillac tow car in March and didn't return until November. *Tommy Ivo collection*

An 18-year-old Don Prudhomme masks off the cowl section for Ivo's twin-engine dragster in his father's body shop. In return for the paint job, Ivo helped Prudhomme install a Buick V-8 in his hot rod. *Tommy Ivo collection*

the rest of the guys I knew because he didn't have to work. He would do a movie once in a while, but mostly work on cars all night and sleep all day."

Prudhomme saw promoters hand Ivo stacks of cash for making appearances. It was the first time Prudhomme had ever seen money change hands in racing besides when buying speed equipment. He thought to himself, "Wow, you can actually get paid to race!"

He also learned that Ivo was a prudent businessman. Ivo babied his dragster. Prudhomme learned firsthand the true meaning of that old racing proverb, "Go slow enough to win." Ivo knew if he abused his cars, this nine-month tour would become nine months of hell. They never lost a race on the entire tour.

Match Races

Fellow competitor Tom McEwen admires Ivo for his racing exploits around the country. "He was as serious a racer as there was," said the driver who became known as the Mongoose when he raced the Snake, Don Prudhomme. "Ivo wanted to win as bad as anyone. He never won any championships because he was always out touring. He was match racing around the country and making money. You didn't get paid for winning national events back then. He spent all his time making money."

At first, Ivo mostly match raced local heroes, but later, with Ivo's guidance, promoters hired in big names for him to race against. Ivo and Don Garlits match raced at least 50 times a year and in the process became a tremendous draw. When a racing accident cost Garlits half of one foot and prompted "Big Daddy" to temporarily leave the sport, Ivo paired with Shirley Muldowney (known as "Cha Cha" Muldowney at the time). Although Muldowney had limited drag racing experience, this

Don Prudhomme
was a car-crazy
youth who wanted
nothing but to go
racing. He had no
idea that money
could be made
drag racing until
he went on tour
with Ivo's twin-motor
car. Here he is
"hamming" it up
with Ivo's
appearance money.
Tommy Ivo collection

opportunity allowed her to obtain a bunch of valuable "seat time."

"Tommy is one of the better drivers I've ever raced with," said Muldowney. "He and I raced on some of the more deadly tracks you could run at. I look back at those times today and say to myself, 'What was I thinking?'

"Being the showman that he is, he was the first to see the potential in a girl driver who was whipping guys' butts."

Always one to keep a sharp eye out for new promotional ideas, Ivo in 1963 realized no one had ever raced against a jet car, which were only making single exhibition runs at the time. So Ivo sold San Gabriel drag strip on the idea of a race between his dragster and a jet car. He told them to advertise it

Practical Jokes

"I'd go into Prudhomme's shop to help him with his roadster," said Ivo. "We'd get into these little battles. He would hold out a bolt and say, 'Put a little oil on this.' So I'd squirt oil all over his hand and say, 'Jeez, I'm sorry.'

"Then he'd wait around the side of the building with a water hose and when I walked by, he'd soak me with water. And he'd say, 'Jeez, I'm sorry.'"

Rat Hunting

When Ivo had some time off in the Cicero area near Chicago, he often spent it with fellow racer Ron Pellegrini.

They would go rat hunting with Pelligrini's friends late at night in a junkyard near the Campbell's Soup factory. "Campbell's would throw all the tomato peels and the other food waste into this dump, so it was infested with rats," said Ivo. "So we had these sawed-off shotguns with powerful flashlights on them that we would zero in on a rat and **BOOM!** Sometimes his friends would even bring out submachine guns.

"Once while Prudhomme was acting like the great hunter with his shotgun, I picked up a metal can and threw it next to his foot. **BOOM!** He jumped right up in the air and almost shot his foot off."

with the hook that should he lose, he would be cooked by the huge flames coming out of the rear of the jet. "They packed the place," said Ivo. "There was barely standing room and it opened the door to match racing in Southern California."

Teaming with Tarzan

Ivo's crewman, John Austin, better known as Tarzan, toured with Ivo for seven seasons. He went to work with Ivo in 1966 as a 26-year-old, but each winter went back into the family concrete business because he didn't make enough money during the season to survive the winter months.

Ivo said his mother created the name Tarzan, because of his muscular physique, but Tarzan is not too sure.

On the first national tour since the cancellation of the *Margie* show in 1963, Ivo and Tom McCourry stopped and photographed their tow rig as it entered Montana. *Tommy Ivo collection*

Lakeland International
2nd Annual Tennessee Spring Drag Festival
★ Featuring: ★

"Cha Cha" Muldowney

"T.V. Tommy" Ivo

Modified $600

1st Round	2nd Round
W—$300	W—$200
RU—$50	RU—$50

Super Stock $600

1st Round	2nd Round
W—$300	W—$200
RU—$50	RU—$50

E.T. Brackets

(0—12.99) Bracket 1—$150
(13—15.49) Bracket 2—$100
(15.50 UP) Bracket 3—$100

Motorcycle Classes

Bracket 1—$75   (0—11.99)
Bracket 2—$75   (12＋UP)

★★★★★★★★★★★★★

2nd Annual Sunshine Nationals Motorcycle Championships
May 1-2-3-4

★★★★★★★★★★★★★

Contact: Bill Taylor 901—774-0800
Lee Taylor 901—363-0865

"When we went back East, my hair was long and I was big and I didn't wear shirts too much, so the name just stuck," he said.

"Ivo was different than any other drag racer I've ever met," Austin continued. "He was very hands-on and drove the car in such a way that it wouldn't need to be worked on much or break a bunch of parts unnecessarily."

Austin said the racing was pretty straightforward, but the traveling had some interesting moments. "Ivo was a terrible tow-car driver, scary, so I said, 'Screw you, I'm doing all the driving from now on,'" said Austin. "One time we were racing on Sunday in Amarillo, Texas, and we had to race in Union Grove, Wisconsin, the next night. Ivo told me it was about six hundred miles and he went to sleep in the trailer. So I drove all night long and it was more like one thousand two hundred miles!

Sensing the Women's Lib movement could spur ticket sales, Ivo asked Shirley "Cha Cha" Muldowney if she would match race him for a season. This event poster touted a race in Tennessee. *Tommy Ivo collection*

In a David vs. Goliath event *(above)*, Ivo raced an exhibition pitting the *Barnstormer* against Romeo Palamides in his jet dragster, which was being driven by Bob Smith. Ivo won! *Tommy Ivo collection*

Waiting in the staging lanes for his exhibition race against the jet dragster *(opposite)*, Ivo skewered hot dogs and marshmallows behind the cockpit. Perhaps if the flames from the jet car were hot enough, he and his crew would have a cooked dinner back in the pits after the run. *Tommy Ivo collection*

"Another time we were racing in Puyallup, Washington, which is south of Seattle, on a Wednesday night and had to be in Union Grove again to race on Friday night. That was like two thousand six hundred miles. I'd just take some white pills, some black coffee, and a few packs of cigarettes and head on down the road."

A Jolly Good Show

Not in his wildest dreams did Tommy Ivo think his touring would take him to Europe. Sure, he had raced a number of times in Canada, where the tracks were narrow and the pavement was bumpy, but the East Coast of the United States was the farthest east Ivo ever thought he would race.

Wally Parks had another idea.

Parks, founder of the NHRA, had been invited by Sydney Allard, a veteran sports car builder and drag racer, to bring a group of high-profile racers to England for three weeks of exhibition races in 1964. "Wally liked pretty cars, and he knew mine were always fast and pretty," said Ivo. "So I was honored to be invited."

Ivo was part of the USA Drag Racing Team, which also included Don Garlits, Tony Nancy, Ronnie Sox, Buddy Martin, Ohio George Montgomery, K. S. Pittman, Bill "Grumpy" Jenkins, and Dave Strickler.

"We sailed over on the U.S.S. *United States*, which, at the time was the fastest ship in the water," said Ivo. "All the cars were put below deck, but because I brought my enclosed trailer, it had to be hauled up ten stories by crane to the top of the deck. My heart was in my mouth. My trailer was strapped to the deck."

On the way over, the U.S.S. *United States* met with the *Queen Mary*, which had gone through rough weather coming west that caused $2 million worth of damage. Ivo was told if their ship ran into similar weather, Ivo's trailer would be pushed overboard so it wouldn't roll around the deck during the storm and cause a hazard.

Tommy Ivo, Sidecar Racer

While racing in England with Garlits, a guy on a motorcycle with a sidecar rode up to us and asked, "Any of you Yanks want a ride?" The bike was one of those that they road raced over there, with a platform, small windscreen, and a wheel to the outboard side. The passenger laid prostrate on the platform, hanging onto a steel pole at the front, with no safety belt, of course, and his legs hanging out in the wind behind him. It ran 112 miles per hour in a quarter mile.

How could I refuse?

As this Brit took off down the track, I saw the finish line go by. Then he chucked it into high gear and kept going. Now, with the point of view that I had, looking at the track at from so low, it appeared to me we were coming to the end as we went over a rise in the ground and then downward into the shut-off area. I thought, "Yee gods, if he turns to one side at the end, I don't know which way to lean. We'll both be killed." So I beat him on the leg to let him know he should shut it down. He paid no attention to me whatsoever and kept going, with me beating my hand numb on his leg.

Well, all's well that ends well. The track was long enough for us to stop. Only then did I come to find out he had a wooden leg and couldn't feel me beating on it. I never did that again.

Ivo, about to get quite a ride while touring the U.K. with the NHRA-sponsored drag racing team. *Tommy Ivo collection*

NHRA stars enjoy the view while traveling across the ocean to England *(top left)*. From left: Tom McCourry, Tony Nancy, Steve Swaja, Ronnie Sox, Ivo, and Buddy Martin. Ivo's *Barnstormer* dragster *(above right)* is hoisted 10 stories in the air and loaded onto the deck of the U.S.S. *United States* for travel to England. Ivo had the only enclosed trailer on the tour; the other competitors used smaller, open trailers that could be stored below deck. *(Above)* Ivo's enclosed trailer (center) is tied to the deck. The captain told him that if they hit stormy seas, he would push the trailer overboard in order to avoid damage to the boat. After the three-week NHRA tour through England *(right)*, Ivo and his friend Tom McCourry rented a VW Beetle and toured Italy, Switzerland, Germany, Holland, and France. All from *Tommy Ivo collection*

Drag racing was a
novelty in England
at the time of the
1964 NHRA tour.
Ivo shot this photo
(opposite) of an
Italian Iso Grifo
racing on one of
the strips. *Tommy
Ivo collection*

"Every night before I went to sleep I'd go out on deck and check to see if the stars were out," said Ivo. "Fortunately it was smooth sailing all the way."

For a bunch of practical joking drag racers, travel by ship across the Atlantic was more like a high school class trip. "We were a bunch of dirty old drag racers, and they put us all the way back in tourist class," Ivo said. "So we decided to sneak up front to see what was going on in first class. But the stewardess told us all the fun was happening in the back, so we stayed back there.

"The trip was magical. We were like heroes."

In England, the group stayed at the historic Sandringham House hotel and raced at six different drag strips over the course of three weekends. "I was going off and touring the Tower of London and seeing plays, but Garlits was always working on his car," said Ivo. "He treated it like he was racing at Indy every weekend. I knew I would have my work cut out for me racing against Garlits. He was so gung-ho."

The tracks were old Royal Air Force landing strips, which were long and wide but rough because of all the patching necessary after World War II bombing raids by the Germans.

Before Ivo went out to test on the track, he replaced his zoomie headers with straight pipes because of all the noise they produced. He pulled up to the starting line where about 200 people were standing around. His car was making about 1,000 horsepower. "I rolled right into the middle of those two hundred people and gave it a good handful of throttle and let the lightning loose," said Ivo. "I looked around and all I saw were asses and elbows running in all directions because they thought the motor was going to blow up."

When they raced at the Blackbushe track that first weekend, 30,000 fans showed up. "We had never seen that many people at a race track before," Ivo said. "And they let the people down onto the track after the race was over. So when we pushed back up the center of the track after Garlits and I made our final run, it was like driving in the Mille Miglia with the crowds parting in front of us."

Even though Garlits' car was faster, Ivo was getting off the line quicker, which upset Garlits. "I was able to better 'read' the starter before he dropped the flag," said Ivo. "He would dip his knees just before

Practical Jokes

In England, new street drivers must display a large "L" sticker on their cars to warn other drivers that a learning driver is behind the wheel. When he was in England with the USA Drag Racing Team in 1964, Ivo secured a couple of those decals and stuck them on Garlits' car.

"He was fit to be tied at first," said Ivo. "He doesn't find humor in things like that. But later he thought it was pretty funny and kept the decals on for the rest of the trip."

he dropped the flag and I'd get a good hole shot on Garlits every time."

At the grand finale event, Garlits refused to run because the track was so torn up. "Wally wanted to choke Garlits because this was the sixth and final race," said Ivo. "I beat Garlits three out of the five times we raced, which I guess made me the International Match Race Champion that year.

"It was a dream to go over there. I'm not sure Garlits had as much fun as I did, but to me, it was just the berries."

When the racing was over and the cars were loaded back onto a ship, Ivo and his helper on the trip, Tom McCourry, began trip number two. They flew to France, rented a VW Beetle, and toured France, Germany, Switzerland, and Italy for four more weeks. "I passed up a lot of races back home during that time," said Ivo. "But I loved traveling, and when was I going to get back to Europe?"

Practical Jokes

Don Garlits remembers Ivo joking around during their drag racing trip to England during Ivo's *Barnstormer* days. "We were in an old hotel around Leeds, which was supposedly haunted, and of course, Ivo was up all night," said Garlits. "He and photographer Jim Kelly were dragging chains around the hallways all night. The noise echoed through the building.

"But he knew better than to pull those jokes on me. I wasn't a practical jokes kind of guy."

Chapter Five

Ivo's Fast 31

Tommy Ivo built some of the most beautiful and outrageous racing vehicles of the 1950s, 1960s, and 1970s. His cars were not only fast but they were often formed like sculpture. He was never satisfied with butting two pieces of aluminum together with a right-angle weld. He preferred that a metalsmith craft a compound curve that looked more appropriate on a Buick quarter panel than on a quarter-mile dragster.

Ivo never took the cheap or lazy way out. He realized how lucky he was to have the opportunity to race cars that most fans could only dream about. He didn't want to disappoint the fans if they inspected his cars up close.

Ivo was a fan of red-orange paint he called "Ivo Red," and he painted cars in that hue during most of his career. Also, unlike his competitors, his cars displayed a liberal use of chrome plating.

Longtime competitor Don Garlits claimed that Ivo often lost to him because of all the extras he built into his cars. "If you look at my cars, they were spartan shit," said Garlits. "So Tommy spotted me a couple of hundred pounds because of all the chrome, paint, and fancy pieces on his cars. That means I could run quicker and faster with the same combination as him every time."

Ivo is proud of the cars he built and drove over the course of his 30-year racing career. Most were built in the same two-car garage at his Burbank home. Imagine constructing the exotic and complex two- and four-engine dragsters in a small home garage.

1952 Buick Super, 1952-1955

1

As a kid, Ivo was interested in anything mechanical. He'd disassemble his parents' clocks and watches and put them together again. He took apart his bicycle and built aviaries and clubhouses in his backyard. But when he turned 16, he knew one thing for sure: He wanted to drive a car.

After looking at all the car brochures they had collected, Ivo and his girlfriend, Nancy, decided that the Buick looked best. So he bought a bright-red Super for $3,000 while on a family vacation in Denver in the late summer of 1952.

As soon as he got the car home, neighborhood friend Tom Jandt suggested he take the car to the drags. "The drags?" asked Ivo. "What's the drags?"

Ivo had never been to any type of auto race in his life.

On his first run down the track, Ivo's Buick achieved a top speed of 66.66 miles per hour in the quarter-mile; not too fast, but after all, it was his first run down the track. On his second run that day, the car went the same speed. "Drag racing didn't seem so good to me, so I came home and started peeling the car apart," he said.

This was the era of the lead-sled custom car, so Ivo began removing chrome and trim, including the door handles and the three beloved portholes. He bought every *Hot Rod* and *Car Craft* magazine he could find to learn customizing techniques.

A youthful-looking Tommy Ivo in his brand-new 1952 Buick Super. Ivo picked the car from brochures laid out on the floor of his girlfriend Nancy Davidson's house, seen here with the car parked in front of it across the street. *Tommy Ivo collection*

"Eventually the car was so spotted up with primer that the other kids at school were giving me a hard time," he said. "Once they even cut my tires. Because I acted in so many western movies, I had to have long hair, so I was kind of strange when every other kid had a crew cut.

"Those were the days before credit cards and loose-lending practices at banks, so I had the only new car in the school parking lot, and that included the principal."

Ivo used to drive past the auto shop with his primer-splotched Buick and the students there would harass him as he drove by. One afternoon after school, using a small, portable sprayer, Ivo painted the entire car in flat-black primer and put large yellow polka-dots all over the body and big pink footprints across the trunk. Then he used heavy wire and fabricated eyelashes over the headlights.

"The next morning when I drove by auto shop, I didn't hear a word," he said. "I looked in my rearview mirror and all I could see were the students' jaws lying on the ground. I heard that even the teachers were talking about the warped mentality of someone who would take a brand-new car and destroy it like that."

Eventually Ivo treated his Buick to a full custom treatment, similar to 1949–1951 Mercurys of the era. He de-chromed the nose and tail and frenched the headlights and taillights. He also had the car painted red, forever hiding the pink footprints that once marched across the trunk.

Thanks to his acting salary, Ivo had a nicer car than any other student and most teachers at Burbank's Burroughs High. Because of this, he was often harassed by jealous classmates.
Tommy Ivo collection

Firebomb

Ivo tried to speed-tune his '52 Buick once and was told that milling the straight-eight cylinder head would make it run faster. So he removed the head and had it shaved ⅛-inch, but when he bolted it back on, it didn't run any better.

Then he installed a see-through glass fuel filter because he was afraid of getting water from his gas tank. But he installed it too tight, which caused it to crack and spray gas all over the engine. It went up in flames that burned his eyebrows, eyelids, and hair, and made a mess of the engine when he threw dirt on it to extinguish the flames.

"It was such a mess when it was towed to the Buick agency," he said. "My mechanical ability wasn't too good during my first attempt at speed-tuning my car."

Ivo drove this Buick from 1952 to 1955. Eventually it became a show-stopping custom. The car was nosed and decked, had frenched headlights and taillights, and featured a 1954 Chevy grille *(above left)*.

Not willing to leave his new car alone *(left)*, Ivo began to customize the Buick soon after buying it. He painted the car flat black and decorated it with yellow polka-dots and large pink footprints to mess with the minds of schoolmates who had harassed him. *Both Tommy Ivo collection*

2 1955 Buick Century, 1955

When his 1952 Buick started to get a little bit old, Ivo bought a new 1955 Buick from his local dealer. He ordered it in white with a red spear on the side. He remembers he paid about $3,000 for it and that it had one of the new Buick V-8 engines.

"I hated to get rid of the fifty-two, so I talked my dad into buying it for the same amount he sold his old Hudson for," said Ivo.

"That fifty-five ran like a son of a gun. It had a Nailhead V-8 and nobody knew anything about them. It had an automatic transmission and a four-barrel carburetor."

Ivo became enamored with drag racing. But on the same day he took delivery, he began to "beautify" his new car by taking off many of the easily removable components in the engine compartment. "I had everything chrome-plated," he said. "I removed the power-steering pump, the rocker covers, and the air cleaner and had them all chromed." He also took steel wool and removed all the paint from the radiator and polished the brass tank.

Ivo chromed his engine parts so when he cruised to Bob's Big Boy on Saturday nights he could open the hood and show off his new V-8. With his V-8, Ivo also became enamored with Drag Racing, but at the drag strip the chrome became an issue. He actually won his class at the Saugus Drag Strip the first time out with the car and was protested by a fellow racer whose 1955 Chevy Ivo had just beat. "So they took the car over to the tech inspection area for Lou Baney to look at," said Ivo. "Lou was a real kingpin in drag racing at the time.

When Buick introduced its new Century with the Nailhead V-8, Ivo ordered this red and white number. With this car, Ivo began a long relationship with drag racing and the Buick V-8. *Tommy Ivo collection*

"So Lou opens up the hood and sees all that chrome and said, 'This car ain't stock.' So of course smartass me said, 'No, it's not. See that power steering unit? It's really a blower in disguise.'

"Baney told me to go home, and don't let the door hit me in the ass when I left." It wouldn't be the last time Ivo would hear those words.

Don Rackemann was the starter at Saugus that day, and he remembers the incident exactly as it happened. "I said, 'You're cheating. There's no way your car can run that fast.' None of us realized that Buicks were really quick. I later found out that Ivo was not cheating. Tommy was the real deal," he said.

The next weekend when Ivo took his Buick to the drags, things went better. "I ran B-Stock at eighty-five-point-seven-four miles per hour at Pomona," said Ivo. "I won my class and set a record, both on the same day. Taking home two trophies for an actor was like winning two Oscars!"

The needle was planted, and Ivo said from that moment on, drag racing is all he has thought about.

Fun, Fun, Fun 'til Mommy Takes the T-Bird Away

When Ivo sold his red and white Buick Century, he really wanted to buy one of the new 1955 Thunderbirds. "They had just been introduced and to me, that two-seater with the removable hardtop was the best thing since sliced bread," said Ivo. "But my parents put the kibosh to that idea."

Not surprisingly, Ivo's mother ended any thoughts of a T-Bird since it was only shortly after her older son, Don, had been killed in a car accident. Mrs. Ivo feared for Tommy's life and told him that her last remaining son would never drive in a convertible because if it rolled over, he would be killed too.

"You see, she had control of my purse strings because I was still a minor," he said. "So I told her that if she wouldn't let me get the T-Bird, then I wasn't going to tap dance anymore. It had actually become an antiquated form of entertainment by then anyway, although it had served me well by getting me in the movies to start with. I was just looking for some excuse to dump it. And I never tap danced again."

One wonders how Ivo's racing career would have evolved if he had bought the Thunderbird. Would he have begun racing Ford-powered cars instead of the Buicks? Would he have built a four-engine dragster powered by four Ford Y-block 312s? We'll never know.

Ivo's first race in the new Century was at Saugus Drag Strip in 1955. *Tommy Ivo collection*

The modifications begin! Ivo chromed and polished many of the Century's engine pieces, which got him kicked out of Saugus because they thought he was cheating. He also installed this two-four-barrel setup without much success. *Tommy Ivo collection*

He explained that the proper technique for drag racing with the new Buick automatic transmission was to rev the car to 70 miles per hour in low gear before shifting into high gear. The only problem was that the car was designed for shifting at a maximum of 50 miles per hour because a snap ring that held a piston inside the transmission would shear and loose parts would fall inside the transmission housing, causing it to blow.

"Well, after the third time I tried to have the transmission warranted by the dealer, they told me, 'The next time you bring this in, it's on your nickel.'"

Once again Ivo tried his hand at speed-tuning when he installed a dual four–barrel carburetor setup on his V–8. He acquired a used Buick four–barrel carb and a new intake manifold, but because he knew nothing about jetting, the car didn't run much better than the single four-barrel. And besides, the modification put him in another class at the track, so he removed it.

Ivo eventually realized that modifying and racing the same car he had to rely on to drive to school and the studios was not a wise idea, so he sold the Century to a friend who fell in love with the car.

3 1955 Buick Century No. 2, 1955

After selling his red and white Buick—and after being rebuffed by his parents in his attempt to purchase a new Thunderbird—Ivo bought another Buick Century, this time in blue and white.

"I just wanted to drive something different and get back to a dependable, unmodified car," he said. "Besides, in the back of my mind, I wanted to build a car that was primarily for racing and not something I had to rely on for commuting."

Because the red and white Century became too unreliable with all its modifications, Ivo sold it and bought this blue stock '55 Century and begin constructing a car specifically for the track. *Tommy Ivo collection*

4 1934 Ford Roadster, 1955

Ivo had already begun to construct his famed T-bucket, but he was impatient. So while construction was underway, he purchased an already-built hot rod.

"At the time, I was totally enamored with hot rods," he said. "So I bought this chopped thirty-four roadster with an Oldsmobile engine. The guy was selling it cheap and I just wanted a hot rod. I never brought it to the drag strip, but just ran it around town and took it to Bob's."

When Ivo began constructing his T-bucket, he bought this chopped cabriolet on the cheap to cruise to Bob's Big Boy on Friday and Saturday nights. But Ivo didn't keep it long. He never brought it to the drag strip and sold it when his T-bucket neared completion. *Tommy Ivo collection*

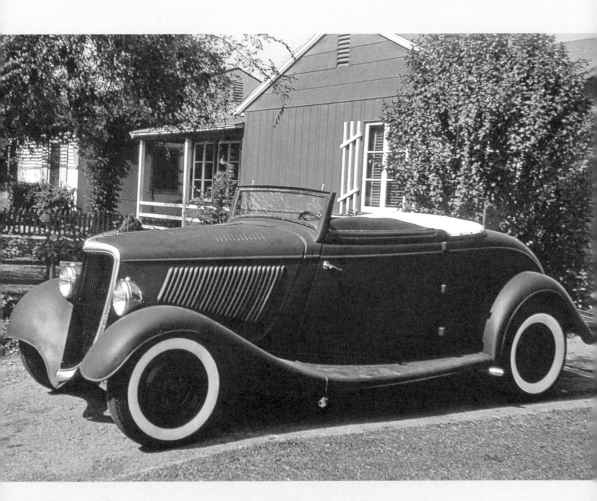

5 1923 Ford T-Bucket, 1956

This is one of the cars that defined Ivo's career as a first-class car builder who paid attention to the smallest details.

"I was over at Bob's one night in my blue and white Buick and Norm Grabowski came riding in with a little Model T-bucket," said Ivo, referring to Grabowski's famous *Kookie Kar*. "I thought to myself, 'Man, that car is the ticket! If I could come to Bob's on Friday and Saturday nights in a car like that, it would be bitchin'!'"

So Ivo walked over and spoke to Grabowski. He admired the heavily modified hot rod and asked him if he would mind if he built a similar car.

"Yeah, yeah, kid, go ahead," said Grabowski. "I don't mind."

"Little did he know just how similar our cars would be," said Ivo.

Soon afterward, Ivo drove to Grabowski's house to look at the car more carefully. Grabowski wasn't home, so Ivo just took out his tape measure and made measurements of the frame, ride height, engine set-back, et cetera. It was an uncomfortable moment when Grabowski returned home to find Ivo lying on his back under the car and checking out construction details.

Ivo needed a starting point, a body and a chassis, in order to build up a Model T.

"In those days, nineteen fifty-six, you could actually drive out into the desert and look around for an abandoned T," said Ivo. "So some friends and I drove out to Palmdale, which is north of Burbank. We drove around and around and saw this old T touring car body that had a yucca tree growing right through the middle of it. That's probably why it was still there, because it wasn't too far off the highway."

Practical Jokes

Ivo had a problem when volunteers came to his house to work on cars at night. When nature called, they would relieve themselves on the lawn right outside the garage door. "They would pee right there outside the door," he said. "It started to smell like a urinal. I told them to use the back of the property, but they didn't.

"So I got a Model T spark coil, hooked it to a piece of chicken wire that was spread out on the grass, and wired it to a car battery. So when they peed, it completed the circuit. They only made that mistake once."

Ivo's T-bucket proved to be a competitive drag racer, as evidenced by the number of trophies it garnered. Ivo said this car is the one he would most like to have parked in his garage today. *Tommy Ivo collection*

After seeing Norm Grabowski's T-bucket at Bob's one weekend, Ivo knew he needed to have one. He cruised into the desert one weekend and found an abandoned Model T Phaeton with a yucca tree growing through it. He cut down the tree and dragged the parts home. *Tommy Ivo collection*

Ivo beat a trail back home to Burbank, where he picked up a saw so he could cut down the tree. He brought the components home and piled them on his front lawn. The body was actually from a Model T Phaeton, a four-door convertible. Ivo cut the body behind the front doors and mounted a shortened Model A pickup bed on the back. He used a Model A chassis because it was a bit heavier than the Model T frame.

What kind of engine would he use to power the car?

"I figured that if the new Buick V-8 ran as good as it did in a full-bodied sedan, it would run really good in the roadster," he said. "And that's what got me started on Buick engines.

"With me running Buick engines in so many of my cars, there were rumors that my dad owned the Buick agency in Burbank, but that wasn't true. I got started on Buicks when I spread all those brochures all over the floor of my girlfriend's house and we picked a car."

It took Ivo a year to build his hot rod, and it actually had subtle differences when compared with Grabowski's. "Mine was more of a street rod and his was cartoonish," he said. "He used a cut-down thirty-two grille shell and I used one from the original Model T. Mine was a little more conservative and his had a big rake and flames painted on it."

Another big difference was in their convertible tops. Grabowski had a cut-down top with a traditional round window in the back, but Ivo, thinking his stock-height top resembled the shape of an outhouse from the rear, installed a half-moon rear window.

Even though Ivo constructed his T-bucket primarily to be driven on the street and to cruise to Bob's on Friday and Saturday nights, he decided

Ivo cut the Phaeton body down to a two-door and added a shorted Model A pickup bed. This photo was taken during construction in 1956 in front of Ivo's house. Because he had such success with his 1955 Buick, he decided to install a similar engine in his hot rod. *Tommy Ivo collection*

The interior detailing on the T-bucket was first-class and set a standard for all T-buckets built to this day. A Cadillac/LaSalle three-speed trans backed up the Buick mill. Check out the small footprints on the cowl—an Ivo trademark. *Tommy Ivo collection*

It really does resemble an outhouse! Rather than go with conventional round or diamond-shaped rear windows in his new top, Ivo chose the half-moon style more common on outhouses. No word on how effective it was for rear vision, though. *Tommy Ivo collection*

Ivo showed up at Saugus one weekend and ended up racing none other than Norm Grabowski, whose car inspired Ivo's own T-bucket. Ivo beat Grabowski by a whisker. *Tommy Ivo collection*

Ivo is awarded a trophy *(opposite)* for his win at the San Fernando drags by track operator Tom Harmon (right) and his daughter Hanna, who was the trophy queen. *Tommy Ivo collection*

to try it out at the drags. "Running fast wasn't really the criteria for this car," he said. "But when a friend whose dad owned the Coca-Cola bottling plant nearby offered to sell me his stroked Buick short block, we were off and running.

"We took it up to Saugus and turned one hundred four miles per hour the first time out," he continued. "And who shows up to race against me is none other than Norm Grabowski. He had a Cadillac engine, and in qualifying we both ran one hundred four. In the finals, I beat him by inches."

Ivo's T-bucket started to win trophies and get attention. Because it was running so fast, he was required to install a removable roll bar and some other safety items. Often, if the other drivers couldn't beat him, they would try to find technical issues to protest his car and get him reclassified.

Soon he was running 119 miles per hour in the quarter mile at an elapsed time of 11.84. Not too shabby for the era and for a car that he would drive to the track, race, and drive home again. He won a class trophy every time he raced it and held the track record at every track the car ran. For a while, it was the world's quickest and fastest street roadster.

"I was an innovator and a pioneer," he said, discussing how he got the most horsepower out of the small-valve Buick Nailhead. "The Buick engine had little, tiny exhaust valves that resembled nails. They didn't breath as well as an Oldsmobile or a Chrysler."

To compensate for this inherent problem, he experimented with various induction systems: four-barrel, dual four-barrels, six two-barrels,

Hey, Where Do the French Poodles Hang Out?

When Ivo began building and racing dragsters, he understood very little about the internal workings of engines. Thankfully he had a qualified mentor, Max Balchowsky, who was the wizard of building Buick racing engines. "Before I met Max, I knew the round piston went into the big round hole in the block," said Ivo. "But he taught me the little innuendos of building a racing engine, like staggering the rings so the oil wouldn't travel around the pistons, or that you point the little oiling hole in the

This cool dog belonged to Ivo's engine mentor, the famous Max Balchowsky. They posed this photo right in front of Balchowsky's shop in Hollywood. *Tommy Ivo collection*

connecting rod toward the cylinder so it would oil the piston from the bottom end."

Balchowsky, who road-raced a series of home-built specials called *Old Yellers*, began by teaching Ivo how to port Buick cylinder heads. "I'd go down to his shop and didn't pay him because he took a liking to me," said Ivo. "But then he'd give me three more sets of heads of his own for me to port. So I worked for my living. I hated porting. Even if I wore a mask, the metal dust seeped in and you could taste it for three days afterwards."

and Hilborn Fuel Injection. At the time, fuel injection was still very, very crude. Ivo said these were not timed injectors, but were basically a metered leak.

"Nobody was building parts for the Buicks back then, so I had to 'woo' manufacturers into making parts for this engine, which they considered an orphan."

The car ran well, and the protests and the scrutiny continued. First, officials made Ivo install fenders over the wheels, so he constructed flimsy cycle-type fenders that he'd install for the weekend. Then, in order to meet the minimum dimension for vehicle length, he was required to add another 18 inches to his shortened pickup bed with a bolt-on removable extension.

Eventually he decided to stop racing the car because of all the hassles that had been thrown his way, but not before winning top eliminator honors at Long Beach.

The T-bucket went on to appear in several movies and television shows, including *The Choppers, Dragstrip Girl*, and the "Annette" segment of *The Mickey Mouse Club*. He rented it out for $25 a day (plus, the production company had to pay for any damages).

Ivo installed this Hilborn fuel injection system on his T-bucket when it was used more for racing than street driving. Ivo said that even though the system worked OK for the time, it was really just a "metered leak." *Tommy Ivo collection*

Ivo drove the T-bucket to Lions Drag Strip, removed the windshield glass and the hubcaps, won top eliminator, and drove it home. In this photo, the car is equipped with six two-barrel carburetors. *Tommy Ivo collection*

Later, Ivo removed the modified engine from the T and installed a stock Buick engine. He eventually sold the car to a fireman from Santa Monica for $2,500 in 1959. It was taking up valuable space in his small two-car garage, and besides, he needed the money.

"Each car supported the next project," he said. "I couldn't afford to keep cars sitting around. I needed to sell them and reinvest the money into my next race car."

The fireman painted it blue, installed aluminum wheels and a quick-change rear, then sold it to a kid in Riverside. That kid brought the car to George Barris' shop, where it was modified beyond recognition. "I don't know why guys who bought my cars always tried to disguise them," said Ivo. Obviously, he wasn't in favor of the Barris modifications, which included pearl paint, chromed frame, and quad headlights.

"It became a typical Barris 'plumber's nightmare,'" said Ivo. "And it stayed that way for a very long time until the owner restored it back to just the way I had it. . . . When he called me to look at the finished product, it was pretty much spot-on." The restoration reportedly features the last pinstripe job by Von Dutch, who had also done the T-bucket's original striping.

Ivo said that of all the cars he has owned in his life, the T-bucket is the one he wishes he still owned.

Whiplash T

Actor Tim Considine didn't want to take Tommy Ivo's advice. Ivo tried to tell him that his T-bucket had lots of torque on acceleration, but Considine was a car guy— why did he need advice?

Ivo rented his famous Model T to Disney Studios for use on a special segment of *The Mickey Mouse Club* called "Annette," which featured famed Mouseketeer Annette Funicello. Considine, who played Spin on *The Adventures of Spin and Marty* and went on to play Mike on *My Three Sons*, was assigned to drive the hot rod.

"In one scene, the character I played had to drive Annette in the car," said Considine, now an award-winning automotive journalist. "I didn't know Tommy, only that he was a drag racer. He warned me about the car's sudden acceleration, but I was already a sports car guy; I didn't need his advice. I told him, 'Don't worry about it.'

"I told all the cameramen not to miss it, because I was going to really 'honk' it on takeoff. Well, I was shocked at just how fast it went. Annette and I almost got whiplash!"

Ivo remembers watching Considine in the scene. "His eyes were as big as saucers," he said.

Considine hadn't thought about that episode for decades until March 2010, when actor Fess Parker died. Considine was reminded of the time he drove Parker in Ivo's T-bucket. "It was during the 'Annette' shoot," he said. "Fess expressed interest in the hot rod, so I took him for a ride. He was so tall that he stuck out of the car's body about four feet.

"He really got whiplash."

Ivo rented out his car for use in several movies. Here it was featured in *Dragstrip Girl,* in which Ivo played the mechanic for the "bad guy." The "good guy" is sitting behind the wheel in this photo. Note that it's equipped with two four-barrel carburetors. *Tommy Ivo collection*

Hollywood's Newest
TEENAGE STARS:

FAY SPAIN

STEVE TERRELL

JOHN ASHLEY

FRANK GORSHIN

DRAGSTRIP GIRL

An AMERICAN·INTERNATIONAL Picture

A GOLDEN STATE PRODUCTION · Produced by ALEX GORDON · Executive Producer: SAMUEL Z. ARKOFF · Screenplay by LOU RUSOFF · Directed by EDWARD L. CAHN

CAR CRAZY!...
SPEED CRAZY!...
BOY CRAZY!...

DRAGSTRIP GIRL

with Hollywood's Newest TEENAGE STARS:

FAY
SPAIN · STEVE
TERRELL

JOHN
ASHLEY · FRANK
GORSHIN

A GOLDEN STATE PRODUCTION
Produced by ALEX GORDON
Executive Producer: SAMUEL Z. ARKOFF
Screenplay by LOU RUSOFF
Directed by EDWARD L. CAHN
AN AMERICAN-INTERNATIONAL PICTURE

6 "Hate" Roadster, 1957

Many drag strip operators, especially Mickey Thompson, who ran Lions Drag Strip in Long Beach, had soured Ivo's enthusiasm for racing his T-bucket. He had to make constant modifications to comply with the rules or else get protested. He wanted to retaliate.

"I figured I'd fix their wagon," he said. "So I built my 'hate' roadster."

Ivo set out to build the ugliest, yet fastest, car he could construct. He started out with a Model A chassis mounted by an old Model T sprint car body he dug out of a junkyard. According to Ivo, it didn't have a square inch of straight sheet metal on it. It was already painted a putrid shade of yellow, and when he gas-welded braces to the body, he left the burn marks. "New paint and chrome were dirty words when it came to the construction of this pile of horse manure," he explained.

It took only about a week to build.

He installed a Model A radiator shell, which was about 4 inches taller than the Model T's cowl, so the hood ran uphill from the cowl to the radiator.

"They had always complained that my T-bucket didn't have enough frontal area, so I gave them plenty of frontal area," Ivo said.

In the back he installed a Model T turtle deck in which he buried one of his father's meat cleavers and welded it into place. "I installed two big ham radio antennas and put foxtails on the top of them," Ivo continued. "I put mud flaps on the fenders, glued shop rags to the inside of the body for upholstery, crossed the headlights like it had been in an accident, and put little corny, sarcastic sayings all over it. Man, it was ugly, but it was fast."

Ivo used the racing engine from his T-bucket.

"So I brought it down to Long Beach and raced it," he continued. "It was at least five miles per hour faster than my nice T-bucket because it didn't have all the gingerbread and accessories on it that probably weighed an additional five hundred pounds."

Not surprisingly, Thompson came over to Ivo and said, "We don't run jalopies here, and that car makes jalopies look good." Followed by the now familiar "Leave, and don't let the door hit you in the ass."

When Ivo began having problems with track management because his T was too competitive, he built this ugly drag car over a one-week period in his garage. It featured the same Buick V-8, but mounted in this early-day rat rod. Note the meat cleaver in the trunk lid. It still won top eliminator! *Tommy Ivo collection*

7 Daddy's Auto Body Dragster, Late 1957

Ivo reinstalled a stock engine in his 1923 T and used it for cruising to Bob's. One night he was eating a burger there when a guy next to him asked, "How would you like to run your motor in my dragster?"

Don Johnson's offer to use his chassis changed the direction of Ivo's racing career. He was now a dragster driver, not someone who had to worry about being able to drive his car home from the drag strip at the end of the day.

Ivo calls this car the Daddy's Auto Body car because the Burbank shop was the car's sponsor, and after Ivo left the team, the shop became a part owner of the car. The chassis was built by a young fabricator named Kent Fuller, who would remain associated with Ivo for many years. It was the first tube-frame dragster Ivo had ever seen. At first it was raced as a bare tube chassis, but by the second weekend, Daddy's installed a fiberglass body for both looks and aerodynamics.

"The timing was perfect," said Ivo. "If it had taken me even another six months to find my way into dragsters, I wouldn't have been at the top of my game because the car's power-to-tire traction ratio was just perfect for the time."

The dragster had a Cadillac/LaSalle three-speed transmission that ran second and high gear only. But Johnson, who insisted on driving the car first, couldn't tell if he was in second or third gear during his run.

"It turns out that he was starting the car in third gear, then shifting to second toward the end of the track," said Ivo. "I could hear the revs pick up down near the lights. So when I got into the car and realized it was too sluggish when it left the starting line, I realized he was shifting the car backwards. We were a bunch of kids with a new toy, but it only took me about ten seconds to figure it out."

Ivo ran Johnson's car for only a couple of weekends, but he didn't like the extra weight that the fiberglass body had added to the car. He knew from his two T roadsters how large a factor weight played. Plus he said the egomaniac in him wanted to run the whole show himself, so they split up. "Partnerships never worked out for me," he said. "I always wanted to be the leading man."

After winning with a Fuller-built car the previous Saturday and Sunday, Ivo was camped out on Kent Fuller's doorstep Monday morning, inquiring about what it would take to order a dragster of his own. Soon, Ivo would be a dragster owner himself.

Ivo installed his Buick V-8 from his T-bucket in Don Johnson's dragster for two weekends. It convinced Ivo he needed a dragster, and he promptly ordered a chassis from Kent Fuller. *Tommy Ivo collection*

Single-Engine Buick Dragster, 1958–1959

"It was so little, and looked so much like a little toy car, that I fabricated a push bar in the back that resembled a wind-up key," said Ivo of the first dragster that he actually owned. **"Compared to the big, blown Chrysler-powered dragsters that would race against my little single-engine Buick, it seemed like they had two engines when compared to my little motor."**

Prior to this time, fabricator Kent Fuller worked for C&T Automotive, which had a good reputation for doing anything a customer wanted for the drag strip or the street. When he left C&T, he opened up his own chassis shop and Ivo was his first customer.

Ivo ran his new dragster with the racing engine from his T-bucket. The T-bucket had a stock Buick motor installed again and the "hate" roadster was taken back to the junkyard after proving a point and winning some races along the way.

Supercharged cars had lots of horsepower, more than Ivo's single Buick, but the bigger engines would start out in high gear and bog down at the starting line; Ivo could dart out in front of them in second gear. "The blown Chrysler- and Oldsmobile-powered cars would be coming after me like those Coyote cartoons with a rocket on his back as he chased the Road Runner," said Ivo. "I spent more time looking over my shoulder to see where they were at the finish line than looking down the track. The catch-22 for the blown Chryslers was they had too much horsepower to start in second, where they would just smoke the tires uncontrollably.

"My single-engine car was the quickest thing going, and the first one to the finish line won, no matter how fast you're going at the end. I set a world record with it when I recorded a nine-point-five-zero seconds ET on gasoline. At that time, NHRA had a ban on running nitro at its tracks. Eventually I got the ETs down to nine-point-one-six seconds. It wouldn't go any better than that."

Realizing that he was not going to go much faster with this car, Ivo began to plan his next dragster, which would have two Buick engines instead of just one. But in the interim, he experimented with a blown Chrysler, like everyone else was running. "The Scoville Brothers had a blown Chrysler they had driven to one hundred fifty miles per hour, but it crashed and killed the driver," said Ivo. "So they asked if I wanted to run the engine in my dragster. All I had to do was make some headers.

"At that point I had run one hundred forty-five miles per hour with my Buick, but at Long Beach I turned one hundred fifty-nine miles per hour with the Chrysler in high gear only—a new world record for speed with the gas-powered dragsters. A fourteen-mile-per-hour step up seemed pretty good to me."

Ivo's first dragster after it was first completed. Note how the angle of
the headers matches the angle of the roll cage; his attention to detail
was already evident. The car featured whitewalls, but still no front
bodywork or "Ivo Red" paint. The Daddy's Auto Body dragster sits
in the background on jack stands because Ivo borrowed the tires.
Tommy Ivo collection

To Ivo, suddenly going 159 miles per hour was a revelation. But he was still well aware that although the Chrysler was fast, it was not quick. "Quick ETs win races, and fast miles per hour mesmerize people," he said.

He ran it at Long Beach, then San Fernando, but it blew up. "Hemis were fast but unreliable at that time," he said. "One or two runs and they would need rebuilding, so I reinstalled the reliable Buick engine."

This was the car that Ivo drove when he performed his first "wheelie." Not that he intended to pull the front wheels off the ground, it just happened. Fuller approached Ivo after a run and told him the front wheels came 1½ inches off the ground. "So when I made my next run, there were probably a hundred people lying on the ground near the

Cartoon Car

"I didn't like decals on my dragsters," said Ivo. "I liked painted cartoons. So I designed little cartoons for my sponsors, like a little mechanic slamming an oversized Jahns piston into an engine block with a sledgehammer.

"Also I always had my name painted on the front of my cars. Roland Leong always painted 'Hawaiian' on the front of his cars, but nobody remembers who owned or drove his cars. My cars were always Tommy Ivo's cars."

Tommy Ivo collection

With the nose and paint job now completed *(above)*, Ivo waits in the cockpit for his fuel-injected dragster to be staged. Don Prudhomme bought Ivo's first dragster *(below)* for $1,000, painted it, and started his drag racing career. Ivo said that Prudhomme bought it on the "no money down, no payment plan," but eventually paid him $500. *Both Tommy Ivo collection*

On August 23, 1958, Ivo's dragster
established a world record of 9.50 seconds,
making it the quickest car in the country.
Tommy Ivo collection

DRAG NEWS
NEWS·PHOTOS·RESULTS   FEATURES

Price 20

VOLUME FOUR—No. 9   AUGUST 23, 1958

World Elapsed Time Gas Mark
Ivo's Buick Sets 9.50 Second

WORLD'S QUICKEST GAS BURNER is Tom Ivo's injected Buick "B" Dragster. Ivo electrified drag racing world August 17 with six sensational runs under 10 seconds, climaxed by new world's Elapsed Time mark of 9.50 seconds. Record was set at Santa Ana, Calif., drag strip. Top end speed on record run was respectable 141.38 mph. Isky equipped Buick has 393 cubic inches and is unblown. Car took Top Eliminator honors night before at Colton, Calif., with victory over double blown fuel burning Olds-powered dragster.

(Staff photo by Don Nickle)

EXTRA!

**Complete Feature
164. MPH Roadster**

20 Pages

starting line to see the wheels come up," said Ivo. "I can't claim to be the first guy to pull my front wheels off the ground, but I can claim I was the first guy in my area to do it.

"I had been running Bruce-brand recap slicks on the car, but I borrowed a set of M&H slicks from a friend," said Ivo. "When I stepped on it, the front wheels came about a foot off the ground until I shifted to high gear. I remember that run and wondered, 'Lord, what am I going to do?' I mean, the car kept going straight and finally came back down when I shifted.

"C. J. Hart, who ran the Santa Ana drag strip came over and told me not to let my front wheels come up in the air again because it was dangerous. So I put a bunch of weight on the front end and it happened again. He told me to go home, and don't let the door hit me in the ass when I left that day."

Ivo took this beauty shot of his single-engine dragster at a park in his neighborhood, now called Johnny Carson Park. His red and white 1955 Buick is in the background. *Tommy Ivo collection*

Serving Country

Ivo celebrated running his single-engine dragster 150 miles per hour at San Gabriel by joining the Air Force Reserves. "In those days we had a military draft, and the army was breathing down my back," he said. "I was twenty-three, and instead of running around foxholes, I decided to join the Air Guard."

Ivo went to three months of basic training in Texas. "I had run one hundred fifty just before I left, but I had to run it two weekends in a row to get the color TV set grand prize," he said. "Well, I was off at boot camp and couldn't claim the TV set because I was saving my country."

Ivo reported for duty in the U.S. Air Force Reserves in 1958 at Lackland Air Force Base in Texas. On the only Sunday he had off during his three-month training, Ivo took a Greyhound bus to San Antonio for the drag races. Here he is standing next to Bobby Langley's Hemi-powered *Scorpion* dragster. *Tommy Ivo collection*

Road Kings car club members—and five future race legends—help Ivo push to the line *(above)*. From left Don Prudhomme (in white shirt), Rod Peppmuller (in sunglasses), Bob Muravez, Ivo, and Skip Torgerson.

Always a jokester, Ivo couldn't resist incorporating a oversized "wind-up" key *(left)* as the single-engine dragster's push bar. *Both Tommy Ivo collection*

The blown Chryslers and Oldsmobiles were beginning to catch Ivo, so he thought more seriously about his idea for a twin-engine car.

At the end of the following season, in 1960, Ivo sold the single-engine car to Don Prudhomme for $1,000 after they returned home from their first tour with the twin-engine car. This car became Prudhomme's first dragster and launched a career that endured for nearly five decades, first as a driver, then as a team owner.

"I sold it to Don on the no-money-down, no-payment plan," said Ivo. "He didn't have two nickels to rub together and would have never gotten started in drag racing if I hadn't helped him. But he was my best buddy and I wanted him to have a much fun as I had driving these things. After all, he paid his dues watching me drive the twin-motor car." Ivo admits Prudhomme eventually did pay him $500 for the car several years later.

Ivo receiving his award from the trophy queen at San Fernando. He said he would sell his trophies back to the track for $5 or $10 each when he needed to buy tires. *Tommy Ivo collection*

(Following pages) A classic shot of two historic dragsters: Ivo's car—now supercharged as a last resort before he built his twin-motor car—races Jack Chrisman's unique rear-engine *Sidewinder*. Ivo said that with Chrisman's lead in this photo, "he must have red-lighted." *Tommy Ivo collection*

9 Twin-Engine Dragster, 1960

Ivo's wasn't the first twin-engine dragster. Prior to 1959, when he built the car, several others had been built and campaigned. Most were constructed with both engines running inline, though Howards Cams built a side-by-side twin. However, one of those engines faced backward so the builder wouldn't have to reverse its rotation. Ivo remembers it being on the ugly side.

Howards also built another twin-engine car, the *Bustle-Bomb*, which had one Cadillac and one Chevy engine; one hung out over the rear axle and the other was in the front. Both powerplants shared a common differential made out of a 1941 Ford rear axle. Its downfall was that the rear end kept failing.

The car that put Ivo on the map *(above)*. This photo shows the side-by-side twin-engine dragster at Riverside Raceway's drag strip on only its second outing. The dragster's wheelbase started at 92 inches, but they kept moving the rear end forward until it reached an 88-inch wheelbase. *Tommy Ivo collection*

(Right) For kicks, Tommy ran one fuel-injected engine and one supercharged engine, which he borrowed from the modified roadster of longtime friend, fellow racer, and auto upholsterer extraordinaire Tony Nancy (right). *Tommy Ivo collection*

Over the Edge

In 1960, Ivo raced his twin-engine dragster at a tiny drag strip, Concord Drag -O-Way, in Concord, North Carolina. His appearance was promoted with handmade posters that shouted his dragster actually needed a parachute to stop!

"The track was level, but the shutdown area went uphill to help slow the cars," said Ivo. "If you didn't stop, there were telephone poles at the end with cables stretched between them to catch the cars. Well, my chute didn't come out.

"I was all but stopped, still going about twenty miles per hour, but I didn't want to hit the catch fence and tear up the car's front end. So I cut the steering wheel hard to the right and went over a dirt embankment. Thankfully my rear wheels got hung up, which kept me from going all the way down to the bottom of the cliff.

"I was OK. Prudhomme drove up with the Cadillac and began to hook up a tow rope. In the meantime I ran to get the camera out of the trunk so I could document the episode."

Ivo's twin-motor would be different. Kent Fuller, who hated odd-ball creations like twin-motor cars, reluctantly agreed to build the chassis.

"All the clearances had to be perfectly calculated before we welded in any mounts," said Ivo. "The wheelbase would be eighty-eight inches long. Just for comparison, dragsters racing today are three hundred inches long."

Standard dragster lengths at the time were 92 inches, so Fuller initially fabricated Ivo's twin-engine chassis at 92 inches. But the tires smoked too quickly at the start, so Ivo asked Fuller to move the rear end forward two inches at a time. They would just shorten the driveshaft each time. Eighty-eight inches was the magic wheelbase that allowed the car to come off the line without lighting up the tires.

Ivo's twin had two Buick engines side-by-side, sitting slightly cocked toward the outside. He meshed the starter-ring gear teeth of the two flywheels together, which is how the engines shared their power. An engine plate was designed to tie the two engines together front and rear so the teeth of the flywheels wouldn't separate.

Ivo reversed the direction of one engine so they would work in harmony. A bell-housing was mounted to one engine, with a driveshaft that connected to an offset differential. This meant both of Ivo's feet had to be squeezed into one side of the cockpit.

To announce Ivo's upcoming appearance, the management at the rural Concord Drag-O-Way in Concord, North Carolina, made up this handmade poster *(left)*. Other ads announced that the twin-Buick dragster needed a parachute to stop, a novel idea in the day. When Ivo's chute failed at the end of the drag strip *(above)* in Concord, North Carolina, Ivo cut the wheels hard to the right to avoid the catch fencing and went over a small cliff. Prudhomme, near the rear of the dragster, brought the Caddy to the shutdown area to tow Ivo out. *Tommy Ivo collection*

Ivo had considered running two differentials, one for each motor, but thought better. "I was worried about losing control if one motor quit running," he said.

At the time, most other twin-engine cars with engines mounted inline had both motors revolving in the same direction, which meant when the driver came off the throttle at the end of the track, the car did a little "sachet" as all the torque was eliminated at the same time.

Ivo's car was different. With two engines spinning in opposite directions, the chassis wouldn't rock from one side to the other when the engines were revved, but instead the chassis would appear to very slightly move up and down as both engines spun toward the center. The parts and technology for reversing the rotation of one engine were not invented by Ivo; twin-engine boats had been running reverse-rotation engines for decades.

"The twin-motor car was the baddest bear in the woods when we built it," he said. "Because it had a better power-to-weight ratio than the single-engine car, it was both the quickest and fastest gas-powered dragster around." Indeed, it was the first gas-powered car to run in the 8-second ET bracket, as well the first to run 170 and 180 miles per hour, winning world records in both categories.

The team of two. Prudhomme and Ivo at their very first drag racing stop—Continental Divide Raceway in Denver—on their nine-month nationwide tour. *Tommy Ivo collection*

To Ivo, the twin-motor car was a large research-and-development project; the learning curve was steep as he went from one engine to two. The toughest part was figuring out how to tune the fuel-injection. "But after we figured that out, we could have put ten engines in a car and it wouldn't have made any difference," he said. This would be a valuable lesson when he built his four-engine dragster.

All-in-all, it was an amazing piece of engineering for a young guy who had spent his formative years not working in a speed shop, but acting in television and movies. The fact that the car worked, and worked so well, makes the feat even more amazing.

Drag parachutes hadn't been invented yet, so drivers relied on drum brakes to slow their cars. "In the twin-engine car, we had big Oldsmobile brakes installed, but we'd go about three-quarters of the way through the shut off-area and the brakes would start fading," Ivo recalled.

So to slow the cars down, the NHRA restricted cars to gasoline only, banning nitro in 1957. That left two camps: NHRA tracks and outlaw tracks. Ivo said that most Southern California tracks—"drag racing central" for the United States and the Summer Nationals—banned nitro. At least in California, gasoline-powered cars were the most publicized and popular cars running.

But according to Ivo, nitro-powered cars would run at least 20 miles per hour faster than gasoline-powered cars. "I was running about one hundred seventy miles per hour at the time, but some of the [nitro] cars already stepped up and were running almost one hundred ninety, which was really fast," he said.

Soon after Ivo started running his twin-motor car, he heard about a guy named Jim Deist. Deist had a parachute that had been used to slow jet aircraft upon landing and he was experimenting with it at the drag strip. Ivo was standing at his doorstep the next day to get one. The parachute worked like a charm and soon after, everyone was running them. Eventually Deist opened a hugely successful safety equipment company, selling chutes, fire suits, gloves, and boots. Ivo was first in line for those as well.

Ivo and Prudhomme took the twin-motor car on national tour in 1960, match racing at nearly every little drag strip across the United States. He would charge track promoters $500 to match race his car against the local heroes. NASCAR was also trying to enter the drag racing market and Ivo stopped by NASCAR's Summer Nationals in Montgomery, New York, and picked up top time, low ET, and top eliminator, winning a new Chevrolet El Camino and two huge trophies for his efforts. At that time, winning a car was unheard of and was by far the peak of the tour for Ivo.

After touring with the twin-motor car for a year, Ivo sold it to fellow drag racer Ron Pellegrini from Chicago for $5,000, which became Ivo's seed money for the four-engine car.

For winning the NASCAR Drag Racing Summer Nationals at Montgomery, New York, with his twin-engine dragster in 1960, Ivo claimed this brand-new El Camino. Ivo's dad would use the car for several years. *Tommy Ivo collection*

Showboat Four-Engine Dragster, 1961

By the time Ivo returned home from his 1960 tour, he had figured out that there was money to be made in drag racing. Ivo believed that if people liked his two-engine dragster, they would love one with four engines. And from a power-to-weight standpoint, it made sense. His rationale was that if you could double the horsepower of the twin-engine car and only add 50 percent more weight, you couldn't be beaten by any gas-powered car.

Ivo constructed his outrageous four-motor, 32-cylinder dragster in the two-car garage at his Burbank home. When completed, it weighed 3,100 pounds, compared with the twin-motor car, which weighed 1,850 pounds.

The four-motor car cost $4,000 of his own money to build. Buick supplied the four engines; each was bored and stroked to 464 ci for at total of 1,856 ci, and featured Jahns racing pistons. Ed Iskenderian provided camshafts, the fuel-injection systems, and magnetos. Phil Weiand supplied all his equipment. "Kent Fuller worked for fifteen dollars per hour to build the chassis, so I bet it would have cost ten thousand dollars to build if I didn't get all those free parts," Ivo said. "If you were going to build that car today, I bet it would cost at least two hundred fifty thousand dollars."

"It had everything the twin had, but doubled," said Ivo.

Ivo used industrial chain couplers to tie each pair of engines together. Both engines on the left side faced backward and powered the front differential; the right-side engines faced forward and powered the rear differential.

On the set of *Bikini Beach*, Ivo receives instructions from the shirtless director. With Ivo's friend Tom McCourry (right) helping out, he was employed to drive the car during filming. *Tommy Ivo collection*

Fabricator Bob
Sorrell, who built
the bodies of all
Ivo's Buick-powered
dragsters, fits the
aluminum body-
work during
construction of
the four-motor car.
Tommy Ivo collection

While he was racing the twin-motor car, Ivo discovered that the
weak-breathing Buick engines responded better with taller gear ratios.
He installed Halibrand quick-change units—2.90 gears in the front and
2.80 gears in the rear in order to get a little bit of push and to get the rear
planted. The front reverse ring-gear unit that made the front differential
run backward had been engineered for the four-wheel-drive Novi Indy
car program.

"The four engines didn't work very hard," said Ivo, "because the tall
gears pulled low rpms. Actually the engine in the Buick station wagon that
hauled the car to the track probably worked a lot harder."

Close-up photos of the four-motor car reveal 16 exhaust headers
exiting from the outside banks of the four engines, but only 14 headers
exiting from the inside cylinders. That's because Ivo, ever conscious of
details, wanted the angle of the exhaust pipes and the angle of the roll bar
to match. Sixteen pipes would not have allowed that, so he designated two
exhaust pipes to run down onto the pavement.

Ivo said that maintaining the car was tedious, but not as bad as one
might imagine. He compared it to an assembly line—a long assembly line.
Because the engines were not "in-phase"—meaning that all four engines
did not come to top-dead center at the same time—the valves of each

engine had to be adjusted individually. "When I adjusted valves, I had to adjust sixty-four valves," he said. "So it took two hours of dragging the car all over the pits with the spark plugs out just to get all the motors done. We couldn't turn them over with a wrench because the crank-bolt ends were hidden inside the body for the backward engines and behind the fuel tank on the forward ones. The good news was that we only had to adjust them two or three times a season."

Ivo also installed a lever on the dashboard that locked the clutch in the engaged position because his leg would begin to shake as he attempted to hold all those clutches down with his foot for too long.

Surprisingly the four-motor car didn't require much fuel for a race. Ivo used a small fuel tank because the four motors used a little over a gallon for each run. Ivo figures that fuel costs were less than 75 cents for each pass.

Upon completion of the four-motor car, the NHRA delivered two pieces of news that did not go down well with Ivo. First, they told him they were banning all four-motor dragsters except for his. "We trust your equipment, so we'll go ahead and let you run," they said. "But from now on, we won't allow any more than two-engine cars to compete." The sanctioning body was afraid that the weight and mass of a four-motor car could crash

As an accomplished painter whose father owned an auto-body shop, Don Prudhomme was recruited to paint Sorrell's newly crafted bodywork for the four-motor car. *Tommy Ivo collection*

Ivo's four-motor car was extremely heavy for a dragster and required a parachute larger than those used with other dragsters. This photo makes it obvious just how much drag the chute provided—the back wheels of the car are actually up in the air by a few inches! *Tommy Ivo collection*

through the guardrails and into the grandstands. Ivo's four-motor car, they concluded, would be legislated as an exhibition-only dragster.

The NHRA also announced that they would begin allowing "fuel cars"—those that ran on nitromethane—to compete in their series. This immediately outdated the four-motor car, which Ivo built specifically to run in the gasoline-only series.

Interestingly, the car most associated with Ivo's drag racing career—and that made him the most famous in drag racing—is also the car he hardly ever drove. Because television executives banned him from racing after seeing the serious machinery he was running, Ivo reluctantly

continued on page 124

Starting 32 Cylinders

Just how complicated was it to start the radical four-motor car? Not too bad, according to Ivo. They didn't have starter motors, so the car had to be pushed down the track.

"Once we got to about forty miles per hour, I let the clutch out," said Ivo. "Because the motors had a ten-to-one compression ratio, when I was being pushed and I lifted up on the clutch, it was like putting the brakes on and the push-car driver had to keep the gas pedal floored."

Ivo said promoters liked the fact that the car took a long time to start because it was a star attraction during the entire process. PA announcers would announce, "OK, Tommy Ivo is preparing to make his run now," and then would make a huge ordeal of pushing the car up the track and then pushing it back down the track, firing one motor at a time.

"You could hear each engine as it would ignite and the announcer would start a countdown," said Ivo. "They'd say, 'There's one, there's two, there's three, and all four engines are running now,' much to the delight and hoots of the audience.

"It had no reverse on it, so we always needed volunteers to push it back and forth," said Ivo. "Fortunately, with this car, we never had a problem finding volunteers."

The good news was that the four motors were so understressed that they needed very little maintenance. In addition, Ivo said the car was fairly simple to start. The bad news was that when the motors needed work, it was a lot of work. There were 64 valves to adjust, which became a long and tedious chore. *Steve Miller photo*

Smoke and Mirrors

If you look at a photo of the four-motor car at a drag race, you'll most likely notice all the tire smoke and wonder how the driver could see where he was going. As Ivo said, it was as impressive as hell to see from the grandstands.

"But it wasn't very dramatic from the cockpit," he said. "The whole car was covered with smoke when you let the clutch out, but the headers down the middle of the car would blow the smoke away from the center, so within about twenty feet, the wind would pick up and you could see without a problem. But I had a lot of fun when people asked if I could see through all the smoke. I would tell them, 'No, I can't see until halfway down the track; I just point the car and pull the trigger.'"

Interestingly, the car didn't make much noise because the motors were naturally aspirated, gas-powered engines with very short headers that didn't magnify the sound very well, so the smoke was much more impressive than the noise.

By the time *Margie* was cancelled, allowing Ivo to race again, the NHRA had rendered *Showboat* outdated by lifting their nitro ban. The four-motor car continued to tour the country as an exhibition racer. *Tommy Ivo collection*

In the cockpit it was all business. The driver stared down four motors and 14 exhaust headers, which actually helped clear smoke from the driver's view. For aesthetics—and to keep the angle of the headers equal to the angle of the roll cage—two headers were routed toward the pavement. *Tommy Ivo collection*

The four-motor car was first tested on the public roads in Ivo's neighborhood. Here, it is pictured at its first track test in San Fernando. The front wheels, fabricated from 1953 Ford truck units, were not yet chromed. *Tommy Ivo collection*

Ivo never failed attracting a crowd with his outrageous piece of engineering. Though TV executives forced him to surrender his driving duties, he was a very visible crewmember and steered the car to the staging area. *Tommy Ivo collection*

Ironically, the car Ivo was most associated with is the car he hardly drove. Still, his acting contract didn't stop him from being pushed up to the Denver staging lanes. *"Pete" Garramone photo*

employed Prudhomme, then Ron Pellegrini, and finally Tom McCourry to tour the car while he stayed home and fulfilled his acting obligations.

Prudhomme was scheduled to take the four-motor car back East but drove it in only four West Coast races after his then girlfriend, now wife, Lynn, told him, "If you go back East all summer long again with those damn race cars, I won't be waiting for you when you come back."

So much for that idea. It was to be Prudhomme's first professional driving job, and of the $500 per stop Ivo charged, Prudhomme was to receive $25 plus expenses. When Pellegrini raced the car, he charged drag strip operators $500 per appearance, of which Ivo received $100 to $200 a week.

Both the *Showboat* and the *Barnstormer* were used in the 1964 cult movie *Bikini Beach* with Frankie Avalon and Annette Funicello. Ivo didn't act in it but was a technical advisor and stunt driver, along with Prudhomme, who also worked as a stunt driver.

A drag racing cartoonist named Jeff DeGrandis rendered an imaginary young Tommy Ivo behind the wheel of a go-kart with four lawn-mower engines. *Tommy Ivo collection*

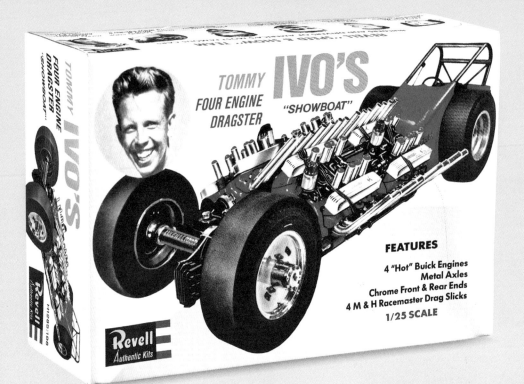

In the 1960s, many drivers inked endorsement deals with model-kit companies. Revell issued this scale version of *Showboat (above)*. As part of his deal, Ivo often lent his time to judge model-building contests *(opposite)*. *Photo Tommy Ivo collection*

"...because JAHNS PISTONS are BEST!"

TV TOMMY IVO

always buys JAHNS, choice of champions!

WHY DON'T YOU?

FORGED and CAST

FOR TRACK OR STREET

Jahns QUALITY PISTONS
2662 LACY ST. / LOS ANGELES, CALIF. 90031
PHONE (213) 225-8177 — (213) 225-1568

Ivo also lent his name to print ads for Jahns, whose pistons were used in the *Showboat*.

Twin-Engine Dragster No. 2 (AKA, The Car That Never Was), 1962

11

Still enthused by the success and popularity of his side-by-side twin-engine dragster, Ivo began work on another twin dragster.

"While I was in the *Margie* TV series, I was not allowed to race the four-motor car, so it was running back East without me," he said. "I didn't have a car to race, so I built another twin-motor car."

This car was also powered by two Buick engines, but they were placed inline instead of side by side.

"I abandoned the project once the NHRA allowed fuel," Ivo said. "So it was sitting on the shelf in my garage when Ron Pellegrini called and said I should let him run that car too. He said he could race the cars against each other for five hundred dollars each, so that's what I did. But thinking about it now, it was a little bit strange; two Tommy Ivo cars would compete against each other at drag strips across the country and the real Tommy Ivo was two thousand miles away in California!"

Ivo only drove the inline twin once, during a weekday test in San Fernando. He made two runs to make sure everything worked, then it was shipped East.

Before he said goodbye to the inline twin car, he removed the aluminum rear bodywork and used it on his first fuel dragster, *Barnstormer*, a few months later.

Ivo explored new body designs for his twin-engine cars. These early sketches *(opposite top)* show the cowl section and the parachute enclosure around the tail section. *Tommy Ivo collection*

While his four-motor car was racing in the East, Ivo built a second twin-motor dragster *(right),* this one an inline twin. Near the time of its completion, though, the NHRA lifted its fuel ban, so Ron Pellegrini drove the car in exhibition matches for Ivo. *Tommy Ivo collection*

Body Design for........ Tom Ivo

Ernie's Camera Shop
Shutter Bug Dragster, 1962

12

Prohibited from driving the four-motor car by television executives, Ivo was going nuts. He wanted to race, but couldn't . . . or could he?

"I snuck out and drove cars a couple of times," he admitted.

Ivo's alias was Jack Snodgrass so studio brass wouldn't know he was still racing. He drove a Pontiac-powered gas dragster called the *Shutter Bug* that was owned by Ernie's Camera Shop in Glendale.

"I just needed to drive something," he said. "The owner actually installed a micro-switch below the gas pedal and found out his [previous] driver didn't push it down all the way, so they dumped him and let me drive it for a few weeks."

On his last ride in the *Shutter Bug*, they ran the car with 25 percent nitro. The car took off from the line so hard that the front wheels came up and dragged the rear aluminum bodywork on the ground. When the front end dropped down, it bent the axle and the front bodywork crashed against the pavement. "Plus some nitro drained out of the injectors, which peeled up all the paint on the cowl," said Ivo. "It was like a steaming pile of junk at the end of the drag strip when I said goodbye to that car."

Practical Jokes

Fellow racer Tom McEwen used to travel with his own pillow when he was on the circuit. "It was a thin satin pillow, and for me, it was like when a small kid carries a blanket," said McEwen. "Well, Ivo got a key to my hotel room, took my pillow, and sent it to Goodyear in Akron, Ohio!"

Ivo sent the pillow to Goodyear because McEwen raced on M&H tires. Ivo had Goodyear embroider their logo on the pillow and then send it back to him.

"A lot of guys thought it was funny, but I didn't think it was funny," said McEwen. "So I went into his hotel room, took the door off its hinges, and took all his stuff—his cereal, pajamas, clothes, all the covers from his bed—put them all in the bathtub and filled it with water.

"He was quite surprised when he got home from the drag strip that evening."

Ivo couldn't quit racing cold turkey during his time on *Margie*, so he developed an alias—Jack Snodgrass—and a couple of times raced this car owned and sponsored by Ernie's Camera Shop. On his last run at Bakersfield, he mixed 25 percent nitro, did a wheelie, bent the nose, and said goodbye. *Tommy Ivo collection*

13 *Barnstormer* Dragster, 1962-1964

Just as Ivo completed his gas-powered four-motor car in 1962, the NHRA lifted its ban on nitro. Prior to this, the only way to go faster running on gasoline was to add additional motors, something Ivo was quite good at.

So he decided to build a nitro-powered car to take advantage of the new rules. Gasoline-powered cars no longer held Ivo's interest. "I was a young lion," he said. "I wanted to go racing at the very top of the heap, with the ultimate, baddest, and fastest drag race cars on the planet."

But the learning curve was steep; he would say goodbye to his beloved Buick engines and begin racing supercharged Hemis. Compared with his reliable Buicks, though, the high-horsepower Hemis had a bad reputation for blowing up. "If you look at Don Garlits, when he smiles it looks like he has chapped lips," said Ivo. "But he's been in so many Hemi fires that his lips got burned off, so he really doesn't have any lips."

Ivo figured that because the learning curve was steep in Hemi engine-building, he would partner with Dave Zeuschel, who had a good-running Hemi engine Ivo could use.

Ivo was a busy guy during the construction of what became his favorite dragster. He opened a chassis shop in 1962 called Tommy Ivo Speed Specialties and put Rod Peppmuller in charge of operations and fabricating. The shop built not only Ivo's own 124-inch race car chassis, but chassis for other racers as well.

At the time, Ivo had the fuel car under construction, had the four-motor car running in the East, ran a race car shop, and acted in the *Margie* series all at the same time.

"I was an industrious little devil back then," he said, thrilled to remember his ambitious past.

Ivo's father, Hans, also passed away during this time, so he was required to take over the responsibility of the heading the household.

The *Barnstormer* was built in record time—less than a week. Ivo supplied the chassis, Zeuschel

You can almost hear the blown Chrysler Hemi engine screaming at high rpms as Ivo burns out with his favorite race car of all-time. Ivo generally did not name his cars, preferring instead that his name be the identifying brand. Like *Showboat, Barnstormer* got its name from a *Hot Rod* magazine writer. *Tommy Ivo collection*

Rod Peppmuller, a Friend Indeed

Even though Rod Peppmuller and Tommy Ivo have been best friends since high school, Ivo has kept a secret from him all these years. Not that there haven't been plenty of opportunities to come clean; after all, they've been through thick and thin together for half a century.

Peppmuller was a varsity football player at Burroughs High School where Ivo was also a student.

"Rod was a member of the Road Kings and he invited me to join the club," said Ivo. "Early on he helped with my welding and he's been welding and fabricating for me ever since."

When Ivo founded Tommy Ivo Speed Specialties, Peppmuller was the fabricator.

When Tommy and Inez got married in 1972, Peppmuller was Ivo's best man.

"He's one of those salt-of-the-earth guys," said Ivo. "I would have had a hard time accomplishing what I did in my life without Rod as my right hand."

And that secret Ivo has kept all these years? It was long ago. Ivo was working on one of his early trailers in Peppmuller's garage one cold night, using a smudge-pot, or an orchard heater, for heat. "I was working by myself and preoccupied in thought," said Ivo. "When I heard the last

Rod Peppmuller does his "best man" duties and makes sure Ivo's tie is straight so everything is perfect for the wedding. *Tommy Ivo collection*

few drops of fuel boiling in the bottom of the heater tank, I realized I had forgotten to refill it with kerosene. I was running out the door when it exploded. The backfire sent a flame over my head and almost blew the roof off the garage."

So Ivo almost blew Peppmuller's garage apart and hasn't mentioned it to Peppmuller for 50 years?

"Somehow I just never got around to it," he said. "I guess he knows now!"

In this photo of Ivo in the cockpit of the *Barnstormer*, he resembles a Major League Baseball player more than a drag racer, which is why he was so popular with fans. *Tommy Ivo collection*

the engine, and any other parts they needed were cannibalized from the inline twin-engine car.

"We started putting the car together on Monday morning, and by Thursday night we were towing it to Seattle for a race," said Ivo. "It didn't even have paint or a body yet, but on Saturday we qualified the car and on Sunday we beat Garlits for the win over a stellar field of cars . . . . It coincided with the Seattle Word's Fair, which was going on at the same time. How's that for our first event ever in a fuel car?"

Despite the time crunch, the Ivo/Zeuschel partnership was not immune to Ivo's practical jokes, of course. "One night I was at the shop waiting for my partner, Dave Zeuschel, who was always late," said Ivo. "He told me never to touch his engines, but I slipped the magneto into place before he got there. I kept ragging him and pestering him about it and he just got madder and madder.

"So just as we were getting ready to leave that night, Zeuschel hooks a winch cable to my belt and hoists me up to the ceiling. My feet were about ten feet off the ground. Then he turns out the lights, locks the door, and leaves."

Ivo hung there in the dark wondering what to do next. If he undid his belt, he would have fallen to the ground in pitch-black darkness.

"I probably would have broken my leg," he said. "Thankfully, Zeuschel got halfway home and had a change of heart. He drove back, opened the door, and said, 'Ivo, you still up there?'

"I was never so happy to hear his voice. But in reality he probably realized that if I hung there all night, the payback for this joke was going to be very severe."

Ivo remembers the *Barnstormer* cost about $4,000 of his own money to build. He also remembers he ran better than anyone in their class with an 8.08 ET first time out, unheard of at the time. Zeuschel's engine was bored and stroked to 484 ci over the stock 392. According to Ivo, the motor made lots of horsepower, which necessitated a different driving style. "If I stepped on the gas hard, I could feel the car slow down because the wheels were spinning too much," said Ivo. "I had to find that fine point so the wheels wouldn't spin out of control."

The car was not yet completed to Ivo's standards and it had already won a race against Big Daddy

continued on page 144

This photo—Ivo's "very favorite"—shows the *Barnstormer* charging off the line at San Gabriel. At the time, Ivo was just hitting the prime of his life. His *Margie* TV series was playing in summer reruns, and he had just broken the 190-mile-per-hour barrier *and* the 7-second barrier to claim both the official speed and E.T. world records as the fastest and the quickest fuel dragster. *Jim Kelly photo*

HANGIN' OUT WITH IVO

THIS STORY TOOK PLACE IN MY CHASSIE SHOP- 1962

STORY TELLER
TOMMY "TV" IVO

IT WAS ALSO WHERE WE WORKED ON THE IVO-ZEUSCHEL FUEL DRAGSTER

ZEUSCHEL WOULD ALWAYS BRING THE ENGINE OVER TO THE SHOP AFTER HE FRESHENED IT UP...

...AND HE'D LEAVE THE MAGNETO OUT, IN CASE WE HAD ANY LAST MINUTE WELDING TO DO...HE DIDN'T WANT THE ELECTRODES TO ALTER THE MAG.

WELL, WE DIDN'T DO ANY WELDING THAT DAY SO I THOUGHT I'D SAVE SOME TIME AND I PUT THE MAG IN.

WELL, ZEUSCHEL INFORMED ME IN NO UNCERTAIN TERMS THAT *IT WAS HIS ENGINE* AND WHEN THE MAGNETO WAS TO BE PUT IN.

HE WOULD PUT IT IN!

TO PROVE HIS POINT..HE TOOK THE MAG OUT..THEN **PUT IT BACK**..TOOK IT OUT..THEN **PUT IT BACK**..TOOK IT OUT..THEN **PUT IT BACK**...

...TO PROVE MY POINT I FOLLOWED HIM AROUND THE SHOP *"RACKIN" MY JAW AT 'EM....*

OH SURE, SO I CAN PUT 4 MAGNETOS IN ONE CAR WITH 32 CYLINDERS FIRING ON MY 4 ENGINE BUICK DRAGSTER. BUT....

...LIKE I DON'T KNOW HOW TO PUT ONE MAGNETO IN ONE STINKIN' CHRYSLER

A classic Pete Millar cartoon illustrates the perils of having two crew "chiefs" on one car, specifically when Ivo and Dave Zeuschel were partners on the *Barnstormer. Pete Millar*

I GUESS ZUCH HAD HAD ENOUGH OF MY JAWIN'... SO HE GRABBED ME..WHEN I WASN'T LOOKING OF COURSE...

...DRAGGED ME OVER TO THE ELECTRIC CHAIN HOIST.. HOOKED ME UP AND....

...PROCEEDED TO RUN ME ALL THE WAY UP TO THE CEILING..ABOUT 20 FEET..

..AND WITHOUT ANOTHER WORD..HE TURNED OFF THE LIGHTS AND LEFT FOR THE NIGHT

HELLO..?

HEY.. ZUCH!..

..YOU'RE ONLY KIDDING...

ARN'T YOU?

HELLO?

ALL THE TIME I WAS WONDERING HOW HARD I WOULD HIT THE FLOOR IF RELEASED THE BELT....

LET'S SEE NOW..IF 124 POUNDS OF JELLY HIT A SOLID OBJECT AT A RATE OF 3 FEET PER SECOND TIMES PIE R SQUARE...

OH MY GAWD! ZEUSCHEL!

FORTUNATELY FOR ME AND FOR HIM HE REMEMBERED IF ANYONE MESSES WITH IVO THEY WOULD SUFFER UNSPEAKABLE RETALIATIONS!

THE ONLY WAY I COULD PRO-TECT MYSELF AGAINST THOSE UNCALLED FOR PRANKS WAS TO RETALIATE WITH EVEN MORE SEVER "GET-BACKS"

(SOMETIMES IT WASN'T EASY)

BUT THE COWARD CAME BACK AND LET ME DOWN!

IVO IS KNOWN FOR HIS OUTLANDOUS "GET-BACKS". HIS MOTO "DON'T TREAD ON ME"

Actors Keenan Wynn and Martha Hyer talk to Ivo about *Barnstormer* on the set of *Bikini Beach* at the Pomona Fairgrounds drag strip *(above)*. Wynn, who acted in the movie, had a passion for cars and motorcycles and had known Ivo previously from his "other" life as an actor. *Tommy Ivo collection*

It's anybody's guess as to which of the three dragsters in this illustrated poster for *Bikini Beach* was intended to represent *Barnstormer*. *Motorbooks collection*

(Opposite) Ivo's run of 191.08 at Lions in December 1962 (with a broken rocker arm, no less), earned a $1,000 savings bond from the track and front-page coverage in *Drag News*. Interestingly, the publication ran a photo of Ivo's previous dragster, *Shutter Bug*, rather than *Barnstormer*. *Motorbooks collection*

IT'S WHERE THE GIRLS ARE **BARE**-ING THE GUYS ARE **DAR**-ING AND THE SURF'S **RARE**-ING TO **GO-GO-GO**

AMERICAN INTERNATIONAL presents

Bikini Beach

in PANAVISION® and PATHÉCOLOR!

SEE THE 'BEACH PARTY' GANG GO DRAGSTRIP!

STARRING FRANKIE AVALON · "ANNETTE" FUNICELLO · MARTHA HYER
HARVEY LEMBECK · DON RICKLES · JOHN ASHLEY
CANDY JOHNSON · LITTLE STEVIE WONDER · THE PYRAMIDS · JODY McCREA
Written by WILLIAM ASHER & LEO TOWNSEND and ROBERT DILLON
SPECIAL GUEST STAR KEENAN WYNN
Directed by WILLIAM ASHER Produced by JAMES H. NICHOLSON and SAMUEL Z. ARKOFF

DRAG NEWS

LIONS

Ivo-Zeuschel Hit 191.08 At Lions

Long Beach, Calif., Dec. 8 Tommy Ivo, driving the Ivo-Zeuschel bln. Chrys. initiated the 1320' of newly asphalted strip by cranking on a real healthy (to say the least) 191.08 run, which needless to say earned him the $1,000 bond which we have had up for some time. Although Tommy's run definitely highlighted the evening, it in no way took away from other outstanding perfromances turned in from a field of competition almost unbelieveable. Low e.t. of the night and a new track record went to Don Prudhomme in the Greer and Black Chrys. with a 8.22 and backed it up with an 8.26.

Top fuel honors went to one of the most deserving crews I can think of, and was as much a surprise to them as everyone present. Bill Alexander, driving Ernies Camera Shops Shuter Bug bln. Pontiac although running real good the last 6 weeks has been plagued with troubles, and have only gotton up as far the last round a couple times, but not tonight, Bill was more than determined to break the spell-and break it he did by first defeating Texas Champion Vance Hunt. The next one was Jack Ewell in the Stecker and Kamboor car which had previously turned 189.41, next to fall to the Pontiac was the Broussard-Purcell Chrys, and finally the real test of the

night for Bill was against Don Prudhomme. This race was so close and such a fantastic match between the two you just couldn't believe it unless you saw it. Bill took the slightest edge off the line over Don, and that was the race right there, and they finished just that close, neither one giving or taking an inch. Alexanders time was 181.80 with a 8.31 e.t. while Prudhomme's 8.36 and 183.66.

The final round for gas eliminator was equally as close between winner Tom McEwen in the Adams McEwen bln. Chrys. against Dode Martin driving the Dragmaster A gasser. And once again the race was won the first 5' off the starting line with Tom taking a very slight edge over Dode, and although Dode looked to be pulling Tom, he held onto the lead all the way to take the final round with a 8.47 and 178.21 against a 8.46 and 174.75, you see what I mean by close, whew!!!!!!!

A run down on some of the competitors very quickly-
Vance Hunt 183.66-8.50;
Kenny Safford-who broke the AA fuel 1320 top time record with a screamin' 188.28-8.46. The car is also the fastest Olds. running ānd is driven by Safford and is entered under Safford-Ratican & Gaidepon Ratican has really done a great job on this machine:

Continued to page 14

DYE ENGINEERING PULLING a wheel stand on the newly paved strip at Long Beach Saturday night. They turned 8.78 & 174.50.
Photo by Kelly & Shipman

Cagle Takes Top Honors At Riverside

Riverside, Calif., Dec. 9. At 7:00 A.M. when the gates opened, the sun was shining over the horizon, which probably seems impossible to those in the L.A. area who were groping their way from one street light to another about that time, but I got witnesses though not very many since only a few hardy souls had made it by that time. Cars began arriving in droves soon after and these weary eyed adventurers told tales of shoveling their way through fog banks or being stranded 20 feet above the highway on top of them. One early arrival swore he hired a snow plow to clear a path and offered a receipt to prove it. On closer

inspection this proved to be a timing slip from Lion's Drag strip and the story was received with 'reasonable doubt.'

About this time the first cars started timed runs and a beautiful top eliminator field began to emerge. Gary Cagle in the nimble AMR turned in a 182.17 in 14.83 seconds with the Brissette-Quincy AMR topping this with 187.50 and an E.T. of 14.42. Now comes the Racer Brown cammed Torco roadster by Alderson & McElvain to post a 176.00 in 15.05.

In the meantime, the hotly contended street classes which were dominated by the SSS cars were making history with

Continued to page 5

Nicholson 1st Place

Sanford, N.C., Dec. 2 Don Nicholson's 'Rebel Rouser' ....the '62 dyno-tuned Chevrolet..was turning better than 121.00 MPH, and that was good enough to take home first place money of $400 in the big invitational super stock drag races on Sunday, December 2nd.

After several hotly contested runs the field was slowly cut down to Don Nicholson in his '62 Chevrolet and Bob Hodge of Salem, Virginia in his '63 Plymouth. With a perfect start, Nicholson pulled Dodge just a little out of the chute....It was close at the half way marker, but the dyno-tuned Chevrolet proved to be too much for the '63 Plymouth. Nicholson's first place win netted him $400. Don Nicholson had nothing but praise for Hodge, saying that the '63 Plymouth sure did run strong. Nicholson confessed he had to stand on his 'Rebel Rouser' all the way. Winning speed 121.62.

Second place money went to Ralph Shaw, driving the hoodless Hinson Plymouth. During the pre-race warm-ups Shaw lost the hood when it came lose and went back over the car earlier in the day. Shaw met Bob Hodge on the line by a car length and that was all he needed. Shaw turned 116.88 MPH with an ET of 12.15.

Continued to page 5

Keeping his safety equipment clean after each run was a constant struggle for Ivo. The driver of a front-engine dragster was usually covered with oil and tire and clutch dust. *Tommy Ivo collection*

In a historic run, Ivo in his *Barnstormer* and Don Prudhomme in the Greer, Black and Prudhomme dragster, face off at San Gabriel in the first race ever in which both competitors had ETs in the sevens. *Jim Kelly photo*

It was a windy day at Bakersfield. So windy, in fact, that the parachute actually pulled the *Barnstormer* backward after Ivo released the brake. Here, he struggles to fold the chute in the shutdown area amid those strong gusts. *Tommy Ivo collection*

Garlits. Ivo brought the car back to his shop to finish it off with an aluminum body, spoked front rims, and a proper paint job.

"At the starting line, Zeuschel would always put his hands over each header to make sure the car was running on all eight cylinders," said Ivo. "Once at Long Beach he felt a cold cylinder, but he sent me out anyway. I ran one hundred ninety miles per hour, faster than anyone had ever run at that time. When the car came back into the pits, he removed the rocker covers and discovered that one rocker arm was broken.

"Zeuschel told me never to mention this to anyone, because they'd never believe we ran one hundred ninety," Ivo continued. "But it taught us that lots of horsepower was not as important as everyone had thought. We eventually changed back to a stock three-hundred-ninety-two-cubic-inch engine."

For being the first driver to break 190 miles per hour, Lions Drag Strip in Long Beach presented Ivo with a $1,000 savings bond, so Ivo started running at all the L.A.-area tracks that offered bonuses for going 190 miles per hour and racked up quite a few savings bonds.

To cut reciprocating weight, Zeuschel once installed a 10-inch clutch assembly as an experiment instead of the standard 11-inch clutch assembly. To their surprise, Ivo did not spin his wheels as much at the start. Using that combination, Ivo ran the first official seven-second run in history on October 27, 1962, at San Gabriel.

Other teams were beginning to experiment with clutch technology as well. Don Prudhomme made his first seven-second run two weeks later when engine builder Keith Black installed the clutch disc backward by mistake. They discovered the tires spun more controllably off the starting line. Black was able to repeat the performance by installing the disc in the correct direction and then loosening the clutch springs.

Ivo and Prudhomme met at San Gabriel for a special match race in early 1963 and ran the first side-by-side, seven-second race. Ivo

Another great shot of the *Barnstormer*, this one with its huge red, white, and blue parachute deployed. When the Wally Parks NHRA Motorsports Museum did a Tommy Ivo tribute in 2002–2003, they used this photograph in a 7-foot-high sign captioned "Drag Racing's Master Showman." *Jim Kelly photo*

recalls that the fans were so excited they almost fell out of the grandstands in celebration.

Zeuschel left the partnership in the early days of the *Barnstormer*, which Ivo ran for almost three years. Ivo wanted to go on tour and Zeuschel didn't want to leave home for so many months. Ivo hated to see him go, because it was a successful partnership. Ivo built the engines himself after Zeuschel's departure, and according to him, the car went faster and faster as the tires got better.

Barnstormer was the car Ivo campaigned in England for several weeks when a select group of NHRA drivers were invited by Wally Parks on the junket.

In 1964, Ivo sold the *Barnstormer* to a friend of Ron Pellegrini's for about $2,000, but not before turning 200 miles per hour in the car just before the sale.

When most of his competitors dragged their cars to the track with whatever pickup truck they owned at the moment, Ivo towed the *Barnstormer* with a matching Buick Riviera. George Barris Kustoms applied the paint to both cars. *Tommy Ivo collection*

14 *Videoliner* Fuel Dragster, 1965

In 1964 when Ivo was on the U.S.S. *United States* on the way to England to race the *Barnstormer*, he met a talented young car designer named Steve Swaja, who attended the renowned Art Center in Pasadena, California. Swaja was Tony Nancy's helper on the trip. En route to England, he drew a streamlined dragster design for both Ivo and Garlits.

"He drew up something really swoopy, but unfortunately, he didn't know anything about wind tunnels," said Ivo. "He designed it to be very narrow in the front and very wide in the back, like the opposite of a teardrop. This would turn out to be a mistake, but at the time we didn't know what we were doing either, so we built it."

The car was breathtaking, with the huge rear tires fully enclosed within voluptuous bodywork. But it was aerodynamically backward. "It was nicknamed the *Videoliner* instead of a streamliner, because of me being on TV," Ivo explained. "A few guys built similar cars, but none of them worked. Garlits did not build one, but he took one look at my car and said, 'This ought to be interesting.'"

Old Ivo Cars

Ivo is often asked the whereabouts of his old dragsters. He sold them all, and most have disappeared, never to be found—or at least identified—again.

"Every time a new museum opens, they ask me about my old cars," said Ivo. "I tried to find the streamliner, because it was such a pretty car, but I never had any luck."

Ivo did locate one of his old rides in Maine, of all places. "This guy bought one of my old dragsters for four thousand dollars," he said. "But as soon as he heard I was interested in buying it back, he wanted forty thousand dollars for just the bare frame and body."

After Ivo ran the streamliner a couple of times, it proved unmanageable at speed, so he sold it. *Tommy Ivo collection*

Quite possibly the most beautiful failure in drag racing history. The reverse teardrop design, proposed by Steve Swaja in 1964, worked on paper much better than in reality. *Tommy Ivo collection*

Ivo ran the car a few times, but it would start picking up in the rear and want to come around when it came to the lights. He thought he could fine-tune the design until he was in the staging lane at Lions and watched another driver in a similar design make a run.

"I was ready to go down the fire-up lane next to the track when this other guy in a streamliner came roaring down the track and lost control right in front of me, hit a telephone pole, and died," said Ivo. "I took a big gulp and a yellow streak ran down my back. I said, 'So much for the streamliner.'

"The tough part was that I was only one week away from leaving on another national tour."

Ivo's friend Tony Nancy also built a streamliner and turned it over on the track. The streamliner era came and went quicker than anyone could imagine.

Ivo's streamliner was sold as a roller to a racer in Seattle for $2,000. "I sold it to Clark Marshall, who probably had as much luck with it as I did," Ivo said. "I wouldn't be surprised if it wound up in the trash can."

Ivo always raced his new creations without paint first to work out the bugs before he made them beautiful. The fine aluminum bodywork more resembles sculpture than a dragster. *Tommy Ivo collection*

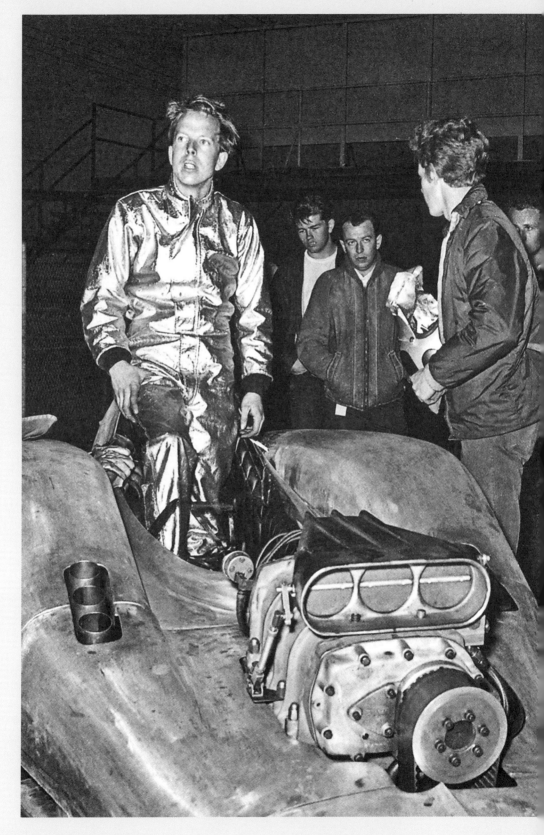

15 *Red Wing* Dragster, 1965

When the streamliner proved unsuccessful, Ivo stripped off all the components that could be used on another dragster—rear end, seats, front end, and running gear—because he didn't have time to build a new car from scratch. Before he eventually sold the streamliner, though, he did reinstall many of the parts he had cannibalized from it earlier.

"We built a new frame in two days and Tom Hanna built a new body in another two days," said Ivo. "Hanna had been hounding me to build a body, so I said, 'OK, but you've only got two days.' He had some swoopy ideas and wasn't a prima donna artist like a lot of the other aluminum fabricators."

Ivo figures Hanna worked around the clock to get the car done in such a short time.

Ivo and his new sidekick, a guy nicknamed Total Performance (after Ford's racing program at the time), hit the road for their first stop in Green Valley, Texas. They arrived at the last minute for a run against Bobby Langley. They didn't even have time to practice, so the *Red Wing* dragster was completely untested when it first competed.

Practical Jokes

Ivo liked to pick on Tom McEwen a lot, maybe because he was such a nice, even-tempered guy. He would regularly get the keys to McEwen's motel room, sneak in when McEwen was still at the track, set the alarm clock to 3 a.m., then hide the clock in the ceiling tiles.

"There were a couple of guys in drag racing who liked to joke a lot, but Tommy was by far the worst. He really thought his jokes out and enjoyed it. Once he pulled a joke on me in a thirteen-story hotel and I hung him over the edge of the balcony and told him I was going to drop him."

Because of his urgency to hit the road, Ivo gave body builder Tom Hanna only two days to build this body. Ivo toured nationally with the car before selling it to begin construction of his 1966 dragster. *Jim Kelly photo*

Total Performance was a little bit too excited at that moment.

"He was getting ready to push me and start the car," said Ivo. "I was in the dragster and he was driving my push car. Well, he got so caught up in the moment—'Hey, look at me! I'm pushing Tommy Ivo!' and waving at the crowd— that he plowed right into the back of my brand-new dragster."

"My dragster rode up onto the hood of the Cadillac and smashed through the windshield," said Ivo. "When he realized what he did, he slammed on the brakes, which slammed me back on to the ground."

"Are you OK?" asked Total Performance. Ivo said it was a good thing he had a full facemask because of all the obscenities that were coming out of his mouth.

Ivo stripped off the damaged rear body section, remounted the parachute "with spit and bailing wire," and surprisingly was able to make the next two runs.

The challenge was to make it to Albuquerque for a race the next day. The Cadillac was damaged and had to be repaired. Thankfully the accident didn't puncture the radiator, but it did push the fan into the battery, which punctured it. Ivo bought a battery at a used car lot and slowly began driving toward Albuquerque without a working fan.

"We'd drive through these small towns where there was no interstate highway," said Ivo. "It would start running hot because there was not enough air

Ivo considered this to be the most beautiful body tail yet, but it didn't even make a run down a track before it was severely damaged by a push car. *Tommy Ivo collection*

flowing through the radiator at slow speeds. So we had a five-gallon water can that we would add to the cooling system and off we went on to the next town. Thankfully, it was raining, so we made it to the next race. But because of the rain, it was cancelled."

Ivo flew Hanna, the aluminum fabricator, to Amarillo to repair the rear of the dragster. "You dog," Hanna said when he saw his beautiful handiwork ruined. Hanna fixed the dragster's body and painted it, but it only lasted a month or two before it started to crack because the aluminum was overworked. Ivo had a fiberglass replacement panel made by a Corvette shop in New Jersey and ran it that way for the rest of the season.

The Lights on Broadway

In 1965, while the bodywork on his car was being repaired in New Jersey, Ivo invited Roland Leong, who owned the *Hawaiian* dragster, to go to New York City and see a Broadway play. "A play? What's a play?" asked 19-year-old Leong.

The two went to see *Oliver*, and Leong was so impressed that he went back two more times that week and even dragged his driver Don Prudhomme to see it with him once.

Ivo had been going to plays all his life; ever since he was nine years old and had a starring part in a play called *On Borrowed Time* with Boris Karloff and Margaret Hamilton. Karloff had acted in several monster movies, of course, and Hamilton played the Wicked Witch in *The Wizard of Oz*.

This is the result of Ivo's inattentive helper, Total Performance, smashing the push car into the back of Ivo's dragster in Green Valley, Texas. The damaged aluminum tail section was repaired and then later replaced with a fiberglass unit using the original body as a mold. *Tommy Ivo collection*

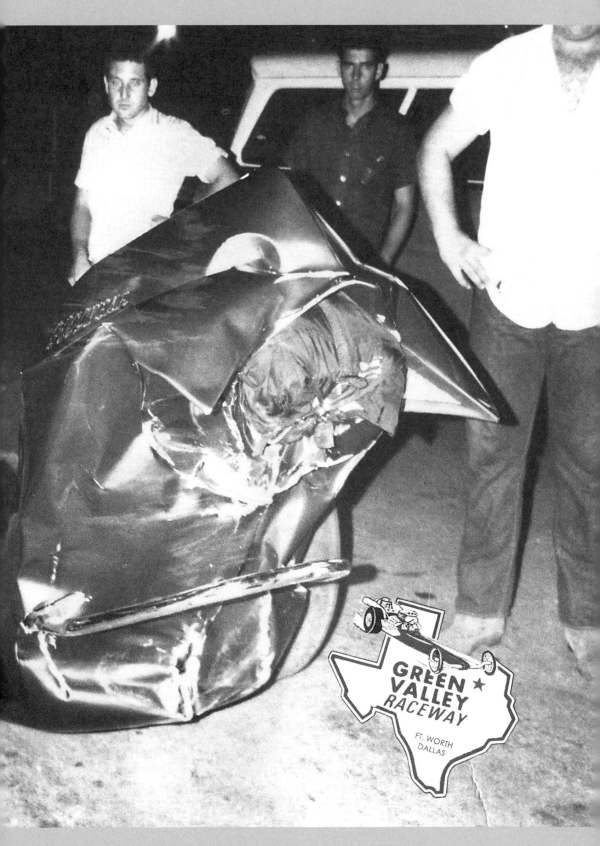

Chartreuse Dragster, 1966

To save money on the next car, Ivo used the fiberglass rear section from the *Red Wing* and painted it green (he referred to the color as chartreuse because it was bad luck to paint a race car green).

"This car was a real highlight for me," Ivo said. "*Wide World of Sports* came over to my garage and filmed me putting it together by myself. I walked in with just the bare one-hundred-fifty-inch frame, and they filmed me putting it all together and getting it ready for the Bakersfield race.

"They followed me to Bakersfield and filmed one of the greatest wheel stands I ever did. It came up about three feet and just hung there perfectly all the way down the track. It must have been going at least one hundred sixty when it finally settled back down to the track at about nine hundred feet. It was an awesome run."

Ivo sold the car at the end of the season for somewhere between $2,000 and $2,500 without the engines. "I seldom sold cars with the motors," he said.

Ivo's chartreuse (it wasn't green!) dragster was a beauty *(above)*. It was one of the few times Ivo painted a car a color other than Ivo Red. Ivo's first glass trailer is in the background as a young John "Tarzan" Austin climbs out of the cockpit. Ivo takes a breather between runs *(right)*. ABC's *Wide World of Sports* visited Ivo's garage and filmed him building the car from scratch by himself in preparation for the Bakersfield event. *Both Tommy Ivo collection*

(Above) Ivo remembers this run at Bakersfield like it was yesterday: "The front wheels went up in the air and just hung there for nine hundred feet at about one hundred sixty miles per hour. It came down just before the lights." (Right) The chartreuse car won Best Appearing Car Award at the 1966 Winternationals. Both Tommy Ivo collection

17 Psychedelic Dragster No. 1, 1967

In the wild 1960s, racers were putting wild paint schemes on their race cars. "Don Prudhomme had his car painted like a barber's pole," said Ivo, "so when I painted my car, I went to [renowned custom painter] George Cerny and told him, 'When I was a kid, I would always draw these amoeba shapes inside my school notebooks when I was bored. Let's do that.'"

The car had a fully enclosed tail section that did not feature the winged style used on the previous two cars. "Some people thought it looked like a giraffe car, but it was pearl white with these oddly shaped candy apple red blobs on it," he said. "It fit right in with the era of head shops and flavored incense."

Ivo ran the car for one season and said it was a fan favorite.

Ivo built this breathtaking car *(right)* during the height of the 1960s hippie movement. It was painted pearl white with candy apple splotches that were actually inspired by drawings Ivo used to make in the margins of his notebooks as a bored schoolboy. Ivo in the psychedelic car *(below)* pulls in front of Tom McEwen's dragster, which sported a borrowed Bebe & Mulligan engine. Ivo won. *Both Tommy Ivo collection*

In 1967, drivers sat behind the engine, so blowing up a supercharger was a very serious deal, which is what happened to the psychedlic dragster at Englishtown, New Jersey. *Tommy Ivo collection*

18 Psychedelic Dragster No. 2, 1968

As cars were being pushed harder and harder to turn quicker ETs, the cast-iron Hemi engines had a tendency to "grenade" themselves with some regularity. This was ultimately remedied with the introduction of the aluminum engine block, but during the cast-iron era, any engine problem at all usually required a complete engine swap.

Always the innovator, Ivo was the first racer to develop a twin–car trailer in 1968: If he had an issue with a motor, he just swapped cars!

Ivo developed a new "lightweight" version of the psychedelic car for 1968 and utilized his 1967 car as a backup. The '67 car retained the familiar enclosed chute and tail section, but to keep the weight down, the new car had no tail bodywork at all. "The new car produced better performance because of the lighter weight and newer technology," said Ivo. "It worked as good as shooting fish in a barrel."

Ivo is all business as he waits in the staging lanes for his next run. In this configuration, the psychedelic car doesn't have the rear bodywork attached. *Tommy Ivo collection*

19 Rainbow Dragster, 1969

The time between seasons was always hectic for Ivo. During the winter months he'd usually build new cars or new trailers. But the winter between the 1968 and 1969 racing seasons was different—it was easier than ever.

Ivo simply repainted both his primary and secondary cars from the 1968 season in an orange-red with a rainbow effect on the panels. The paint featured actual glass fragments that reflected sunlight or spotlights.

The 1968 season ended with a bang, however. Ivo was attempting to qualify both cars at Indy when the clutch blew in his full-bodied car as it was going through the lights during his qualifying run. Essentially cut in half, the car qualified but was so badly damaged that it couldn't compete in the finals the next day. Ivo attempted to use his unqualified second car in the finals, but the NHRA said no.

"Nobody was running two-car operations at the time, so there was no precedent for my request," said Ivo. "So I tried to rationalize with them. I said, 'I can change tires if they blow, I can change the front end if it gets bent, I can change the motor if it blows, so all I want to do is change it all at once!'"

The NHRA officials had a half-hour session among themselves and concluded that the roll bar hoop over the driver's head from the qualified car had to be on the car entered in the finals. In theory this was possible, but would require a lot of overnight fabrication and welding, so Ivo took a pass. "I had already totaled one dragster and had quite a few match races booked for the rest of the season, so I decided not to risk it," he said.

Ivo's 1968 car *(above)* was painted in a base of red with a rainbow of colors and actual glass chips across the nose. This car was cut in half when the clutch exploded at Indy. Ivo sits in the cockpit of the rainbow car *(opposite)* as his red Cadillac push car tends to him in the staging area. *Both Tommy Ivo collection*

20 RCS Parallelogram Dragster, 1970

As his backup car for the 1970 season, Ivo used the same old tired tail section from the 1967 car on a completely new chassis after the clutch disaster at Indy. Then he built an entirely new primary car that featured a new front-end design called a Parallelogram developed by Race Car Specialties.

The car just wouldn't handle, though, according to Ivo. "I felt it was dangerous, so I ordered a new Don Long chassis midseason," he said.

Until it arrived, he ran the backup car, which required the entire tow rig to be unloaded at every stop. It was a busy season.

After receiving the new car from Don Long, Ivo sold the Parallelogram car to Atlanta Speed Shop in Georgia, telling them it didn't handle. "I told them there was something seriously wrong with the handling and that they should 'front-half' it, which means they should install a conventional front suspension and frame," said Ivo. "Well, they didn't believe me, so the car crashed and the guy who was driving it became a paraplegic."

Ivo's new Parallelogram car is in the foreground. His backup—the same old tired tail section from the 1967 car on a completely new chassis after the clutch disaster at Indy—is in the background. When the Parallelogram car proved unreliable, Ivo used the backup full-time until his new Don Long car arrived. *Tommy Ivo collection*

21 Last Front-Engine Dragster, 1971

Ivo took the Don Long car from 1970 and had a full body installed on it for the 1971 season. According to Ivo, this was the "swoopiest"-looking dragster he had built yet. Each car got more and more stylish in the tail section, and to him, this one took the cake.

It was also painted in his favorite shade of Ivo Red. "Except for the chartreuse car, and a blue dragster I had to build for a model car company, all my cars were either red or orange or orange and yellow," he said. "I'm an orange person; it's my favorite color. It's also flashy for race cars."

Ivo built this car, not knowing it would be his last front-engine car, and proudly brought it to the Winternationals. Pulling into the same meet was Don Garlits with his new rear-engine car. He had been secretly building this new design in his Florida shop, far away from prying eyes, cameras, and journalists.

Initially there was talk that Garlits' new car would not be allowed to race, but officials eventually gave in. It was so new and untested that it did not even have a rear wing installed yet.

Then Garlits had the audacity to win the Winternationals with the new car.

Ivo's last front-engine car is now a barn find in Maine. Ivo said the owner paid $4,000 for it, but when Ivo expressed interest in purchasing it, the asking price shot up to $40,000. *Tommy Ivo collection*

Ivo and his then wife, Inez, wearing her race track miniskirt and boots, helped douse Ivo and crew with bug spray at a Georgia track. Inez was quite the looker and developed her own fan following at the race tracks. *Tommy Ivo collection*

This is the last dragster—but not the last race car—in which Ivo would sit behind the engine. Ivo ran this car in the 210–220-mile-per-hour range and beat Garlits every once in a while, but Garlits' new rear-motor car was more consistent than any of the now outdated front-motor cars. Ivo ordered a new Woody Gilmore chassis that was delivered when he arrived home from his national tour.

Bleach Burnout

"A guy with M&H Tires told me that I could get better traction if I poured Clorox bleach under the tires before I did a burnout. That's why and when they started doing burnouts" said Ivo.

"'It gives you better bite when you nail it," he explained. "It was similar to when a boxer puts rosin on his feet for better traction in the ring. It would allow you to use a stronger clutch because the tires hooked up quicker when you staged the car right on top of the hot rubber you had just laid down."

Eventually VHT came out with a specially developed traction compound called TrackBite, and bleach went back into the laundry.

GIANT 21 x 28 TOM IVO POSTER

**Mail to: MERCURY, Dept. MT,
P.O. Box 6346, Providence, R.I. 02904**
I enclose $1.50 (Check or money order. No cash or stamps please)
for the Tom Ivo Poster (in a mailing tube).

**While
they last!**

$1.50

Includes postage
and handling.

NAME_____

ADDRESS_____

CITY_____STATE_____ZIP_____

For a proof of purchase and a modest S&H
fee, Fram oil filters offered a spectacular
poster of "Tom Ivo" in the 1971 car.

"It's not that he ran so much faster than everybody else, but he just ran consistently," said Ivo. "I looked at him running down the strip and he was all over the place. I thought to myself, 'How is he going to run that thing at all those little back-alley tracks all over the country?' But as soon as he won the Winternationals, he went to a World of Outlaws sprint car race and watched how their rear wings worked. Once he put a big wing on his car, it became more stable and unbeatable."

Ivo was forced to race his front-engine dragster for the rest of the season knowing that the design was the last of a breed. "What could I do? Stop racing for a month-and-a-half to build a new car? I'd probably miss twelve appearances, and that would wipe out my profit for the year.

"I felt like I was in a Chinese finger trap," he said. "Here I was, ready to go on tour within two weeks, and Garlits shows up with that damn rear-motor car. And he whipped me like a dog all year."

Ivo was running in the 210- to 220-mile-per-hour range and could beat Garlits once in a while, but the 1971 season was a humbling experience for him. As soon as Ivo realized he needed to have a rear-engine design in order to compete, he ordered a Woody Gilmore chassis, which was waiting for him in November when he returned home from his tour. AMT made a model of this car that was re-released in 2009.

Practical Jokes

"Once Garlits and I were racing in Muncie, Indiana, which was a terrible little track," said Ivo. "It was the last round and he started to notice water drops on his goggles. It was starting to rain.

"He shut down his engine just as the starter was getting ready to give us the green. But it wasn't raining on my side of the track. I ran as straight as an arrow.

"Garlits got out of the car and walked over to my side of the track and it was bone dry!

"This was a practical joke that I had nothing to do with!"

AMT issued this model of the 1971 car. For their dealer ads, the kit maker featured a caricature of Ivo. The model was re-released in 2009.

Rear-Engine Dragster No. 1, 1972

Ivo's debut with his new rear-engine car was spectacular. When all the other competitors were running an ET of 6.20, maybe even 6.10 seconds, he ran 5.97 seconds, the first dragster in the world to go that quickly.

One week later two more cars did it at the World Finals Nationals in California, but Ivo was the first.

Drag News ran a huge headline announcing his record. Much to Ivo's delight, on the starting line at the Winternationals the following spring of 1972, Wally Parks and Tom Shedden, the president of Cragar Industries, presented him with a painting depicting his likeness for being the first member of the Cragar Five-Second Club. Today it hangs on the Five-Second Club wall at Cragar headquarters along with paintings of the other 16 club members.

Ivo seems to remember that his chassis was about 190 to 200 inches. Also, the primitive steering from the front-engine design was replaced with a rack–and–pinion unit.

"The rear-engine design was so much safer than the front-engine car," said Ivo, "It saved a lot of lives over the years and was a quantum leap for dragster design."

Still a stickler for the smallest details, Ivo again enclosed the back of the car with a small body that swept up the wing struts to the bottom of the rear wing. It didn't have anything to do with the aerodynamics, but made his rear-engine car stand out from the other competitors.

Ivo's historic run in his first rear-engine car made national headlines in *Drag News*. *Tommy Ivo collection*

Ivo proudly poses with his first rear-engine racer. His debut with the car was historic. When other cars were running 6.10 to 6.20 ETs, Ivo ran 5.97 during his first season with the car. It was the first dragster in the world to go that quickly. At 200 inches, it was also the longest Ivo had driven. *Tommy Ivo collection*

Ivo pops the chute after a good run. *Tommy Ivo collection*

Ivo is honored by Wally Parks (left) and Tom Shedden, president of Cragar, as the first driver in Cragar's Five-Second Club. The painting today hangs in Ivo's den. *Tommy Ivo collection*

Ivo, wife Inez, and crewman Tarzan (with cigarette and champagne) celebrate after winning the Grand Championship at New England Dragway. *Gregory Safchuk photo*

Ivo did some of the most amazing fire burnouts *(below)* with this car. He would have a crewmember pour 5 gallons of gasoline on the pavement, light it, and give him the signal to go. This photo is a side view of the same burnout depicted on the front cover. *Tom West photo*

Practical Jokes

It was no secret among racers that Ivo slept during the day and was awake at night. Sometimes at night he worked on his dragsters in the motel parking lot; other times he pulled practical jokes on fellow racers.

One night he and John "Tarzan" Austin were standing in a motel parking lot when Ivo noticed that all the tow rigs—his included—were virtually identical Chevrolet or GMC dually pickups. The only difference was that they were all different colors.

Hmmm. Ivo had a plan. He and Tarzan grabbed some wrenches and took the hoods off all the trucks, then swapped them onto trucks of a different color. When the racers walked out to the parking lot in the morning, they instantly noticed that all their trucks had different color hoods—green trucks had white hoods and blue trucks had red hoods.

"IVO!" they yelled, knowing there was only one person who would do this.

Ivo was fast asleep in his room.

Ivo kids around with his new rear-engine dragster in his garage. The car is where Ivo's master bath suite and trophy room are now located. *Tommy Ivo collection*

23

Rear-Engine Dragster No. 2, 1973

In 1973, Ivo used the same Woody Gilmore chassis as he used in his 1972 car. The color Ivo chose to paint this dragster, however, was unusual. It was only the second time he painted any of his cars a color other than some shade of Ivo Red, choosing blue because model company AMT, who had produced a model of the first rear-engine car, wanted to get a second use of the mold. They wanted to use a blue plastic, and even though Ivo hated blue, the sponsorship dollars convinced him to think otherwise.

Ivo was one of three drivers (the other two being Garlits and Prudhomme) who ran under the Wynn's banner that year. He received a $6,000 sponsorship, his largest up to that time.

Ivo did change the front of the body, streamlining it, and added wheel fairings for the first time. "It ran good and we raced it in a whole bunch of races," he said, "but there were no big stories with this car."

(Above) Ivo is still up to his old tricks. Track operators eventually banned him from pouring gasoline onto the pavement for fire burnouts because it permanently damaged the surface. *Steve Miller photo.* One of the only race cars that Ivo painted a color other than red, this blue dragster *(right)* was made into a model kit by AMT. It's the same Woody Gilmore chassis as the previous year's car, but with swoopy new bodywork and front-wheel fairings. *Tommy Ivo collection*

24

Rear-Engine Dragster No. 3, 1974

For several years, Ivo had a second base of operations in Cleveland, Ohio. There, a race car fabricator named Larry Sikora would patch and repair Ivo's cars when they broke.

"Why don't you let me build a car for you?" asked Sikora. "I'll just give it to you."

Ivo thought about it for at least a second before responding, "Sure, why not."

Sikora was not like Woody Gilmore, who had a Henry Ford–type assembly line and several chassis under construction at the same time. Sikora built one chassis at a time.

"He copied a lot of the Gilmore design from my other car, like the basic dragster requirements that all the chassis builders had to adhere to, such as roll cage design," said Ivo. "But he moved the rear wing down lower and farther back than Gilmore did. He said it gave the car a swoopy, more 'darty' look. So I said, 'Bitchin'. Go for it.' At the time, who knew?

"We now know that was the wrong thing to do. If you look at dragsters today, the wings are two stories in the air in order to grab clean air from way above the car."

By the fourth run at the first event of the year, Ivo would look death straight in the eye from this car (see Prologue).

Front Wheel Fairings

Always on the cutting edge of dragster design, Ivo took a page out of jet aircraft design and covered his car's front wheels with fairings. They were designed with more fairing behind the center of the wheel than in front of it, so their influence on aerodynamics would be minimal.

"If anything, I wanted to make the car to go straighter," he said. "The older steering design was so sloppy that you just got used to the slop. But these rack-and-pinion units turned when you breathed on them. These fairings helped to keep the car heading straight, especially if the front end was in the air."

Larry Sikora of Cleveland built this chassis for Ivo based on the
Woody Gilmore design, except it had a lower rear wing. The design,
the colors, the graphics, and the wheel fairings make the car a
showpiece, but that lower rear wing design used up eight of Ivo's
nine lives. *Tommy Ivo collection*

25 Nationwise Rod Shop Dragster, 1975

In the mid-1970s, Ivo's interest in drag racing began to lose its edge. At 36 years old, he had just gotten married to Inez and didn't want to work on cars as much. "I wanted to play house with my new bride," he said. By this time he had spent over a decade on the road. "I was getting tired of living in hotel rooms."

It was also the first time Ivo had a major sponsor. Nationwise Rod Shop had ponied up $40,000 to put their name on his car. Ivo welcomed the additional resources, but regretted his loss of freedom as a freelance driver. The Rod Shop required that Ivo run in six NHRA National events. To him, that represented a loss of 12 weekend appearances at $1,250 to $1,500 each, not counting the many weekday races he'd miss. "In my mind, I was just trading dollars," said Ivo. "Plus the national events were harder on cars and tore up more equipment.

"But I was most unhappy when [Nationwise] pulled Tommy Ivo off the nose of the car and put it in little letters on the cockpit." Ivo felt he lost some of his identity. He always wanted to keep his "brand" front and center so fans and the media had no question about whose car was on the track.

The Rod Shop also wouldn't allow Ivo to paint his car in the traditional Ivo Red. The paint scheme of red, white, blue, and yellow was dictated by the sponsor, as were uniform designs. "I asked them, 'Who owns this car, anyway?'" said Ivo. "They said, 'We do.'"

The chassis of this car was built by San Francisco–area builder Ron Attebury, who Ivo said was very good at fabricating dragster chassis and other cars and parts.

Ivo recalled that the car ran well with nothing terribly exciting happening on the strip during the season. But this was a different kind of season. "I became disenchanted because I liked being the captain of my own ship," he said. "Because I had fairly recently gotten married and a lot of things were changing in my life, I was ready to drive something new. I had driven front- and rear-engine dragsters for so long and everyone else was changing over to Funny Cars. I wanted one of those."

This is Ivo's last dragster before switching to a Funny Car. The chassis of the Nationwise Rod Shop dragster was built by San Francisco fabricator Ron Attebury. Ivo became disillusioned with racing during the time he drove this dragster. His name was pulled off the nose by his sponsor and he was looking forward to having a grand new adventure in racing with his upcoming Funny Car. *Tommy Ivo collection*

26 Funny Car No. 1, 1976

In 1976, Ivo told Nationwise Rod Shop that the next year he wanted to drive a Funny Car instead of a dragster. He had the conversation while standing and talking with a sponsor representative at the guardrail of a drag strip. Just then, a Funny Car came by them and burst into flames.

"You sure you want to drive one of those?" asked the sponsor.

Ivo was committing to once again get behind the engine. Gone would be the safety of sitting in front of the engine. And where dragsters were about 200 inches in length at the time, the Funny Cars were built on an ornery 110-inch wheelbase, about half the length. "When you batted a Funny Car, they went every which way but straight," said Ivo.

Jaime Sarte built the chassis for Ivo's first three Funny Cars.

Ivo's friend Kenny Safford, who himself drove the Mr. Norm's Funny Car for a while, accompanied Ivo to Fremont Dragway to help him fire up his new Funny Car for the first time. He mistakenly crossed a couple of ignition wires and "banged" the blower (igniting the wrong cylinder and backfiring through the intake manifold), so they couldn't test the car.

"So the first time I ever ran this car was in a race," Ivo said, "I made it to the final round and got beaten by Tom McEwen. The headlines read, 'Ivo's Debut Spoiled,' but it was a pretty good show to make it into the finals the very first time I had ever driven a Funny Car."

Bored with dragsters Ivo sought the excitement of something a little more ornery, so he built his first Funny Car, which was almost half the length of his 200-inch dragster and put Ivo back behind the engine. The Dodge Dart had a Jaime Sarte chassis and was sponsored by Nationwise. *Tommy Ivo collection*

Ivo once did some body repair on his Funny Car, but the cool air that night did not allow the resin and fiberglass cloth to set properly. The next day, as Ivo approached the lights on a run, the windshield caved in and slugged Ivo in the face, leaving him bleeding severely while lifting the top and the back half of the body off. *Tommy Ivo collection*

Since Dodge at the time didn't make a suitable Funny Car body, Ivo used sister company Plymouth's Duster body and disguised it as a Dart. Here, at Blaney, South Carolina, Ivo and his long-hair team, crew chief Terry Howland (left) and Greg Lang (right), receive their award for winning the NHRA regional points race.

When he ran the car at Englishtown, New Jersey, the blower blew off and took the windshield and the top of the body off with it. Ivo was not injured and started repairing the body as quickly as possible, using fiberglass cloth, epoxy, and body filler. But because it was cold that night, the adhesives didn't set up correctly. "So the next day during a run, the roof supports broke and the whole windshield came in on me," he said. "The whole back of the car fell off in the lights. I still have the goggles that shattered when that happened. I could feel the pain of those goggles on my face for a week."

Ivo became known for doing long burnouts in the Funny Car. Sometimes, for the pleasure of the fans, he would do a nearly quarter-mile-long burnout then charge in reverse at a high rate of speed back to the starting line. Another crew chief once came up to Ivo and jokingly told him that he might have just broken the reverse Funny Car speed record. "Going backward was hell on those transmission gears," said Ivo. "I'm lucky that I got away with only tearing up the reverse gears one time."

Ivo's sponsor had a relationship with Dodge, but the automaker had no suitable body styles that year. Instead they used a Duster body from Plymouth. As the fiberglass body was being built, they changed the front and tilted the nose back a little bit and did their best to disguise it as a Dodge Dart.

"Funny cars were new and exciting," said Ivo. "I was all bright-eyed and bushy-tailed and happy as a lark because these cars were brand-new."

At the far end of the Orange County drags strip, Ivo performed his signature flaming burnout *(opposite)*. He removed his parachute, lathered up the rear of the car body with Vaseline, lit 5 gallons of gasoline, and hit the throttle. In 2008, Ivo met Robert Butler, a serious Tommy Ivo fan. Butler had the photo of the flaming Duster Funny Car tattooed on his arm *(right)*. Both Tommy Ivo collection

Ivo later discovered his 1978 Duster body outside a muffler shop in Palm Springs, California *(right)*. He said it had been repaired so many times that the fiberglass was an inch thick in some areas. *Tommy Ivo collection*

27 Funny Car No. 2, 1977

Ivo's second year in Funny Cars alternated between Dodge Dart and Dodge Cordoba bodies. His sponsor, Nationwise Rod Shop, again gave him $40,000 but tried to recoup some of their investment by "selling" Ivo's sponsorship to some of their product vendors for a total of nearly $1 million. At the time Nationwise Rod Shop was a Pep Boys–type store that sponsored a complete racing team of various cars in different classes at the drags, captained by Ivo as their star.

"So when they didn't get what they wanted out of their racing sponsorship deal for the next year, I got divorced from the Rod Shop and took back the reigns to run my Funny Car," said Ivo. "I went to the world finals at the end of that year and it was the best the car had ever run.

"We almost won that race."

Ivo said his three-man crew didn't need to rebuild the engines between each run. They took the heads off a lot, but it wasn't like it is today, where a driver makes one run and the engine is dead.

Ivo would regularly run in eight-car fields, where he and the others would race hard then all go out to dinner and take over a restaurant. "The camaraderie was really there in those days," he said. "It isn't like that anymore."

Ivo had another divorce that year—his marriage from Inez ended, which he said wasn't cheap.

Ivo's second Funny Car also had a chassis built by Jaime Sarte. He again received sponsorship from the Rod Shop but was told it would be his last. *Tommy Ivo collection*

Visually, the graphics on all of Ivo's race cars were spectacular, but this red, white, and blue scheme is particularly stunning *(above)*. Here it is waiting to qualify at Ontario Motor Speedway. *Tommy Ivo collection*

Ivo's barn-find Funny Car body *(above)*. This was the spare body for Ivo's 1977 Funny Car. Thirty years after selling it, he received this photo of the body as it sits today somewhere near Columbus, Ohio. *Tommy Ivo collection*

These were tough days for Ivo *(left)*. He would lose his Rod Shop sponsorship and his marriage to Inez would soon come to an end. *Courtesy The American Hot Rod Foundation (ahrf.com)/Tommy Ivo collection*

28 Funny Car No. 3, 1978

In 1978 Ivo ran a Funny Car with a Plymouth Arrow body because they were much more aerodynamic than the Dodge bodies then available. "They also looked twice as good as those other two patched-up orphan messes I ran the previous two years," he added. "Plus I was back calling the shots again."

It was a transition year for Ivo, who had lost his major sponsor for the 1978 season and was still getting over his failed marriage. He had to truck all his belongings from his Cleveland house back to Burbank and at the same time was building the new Arrow and preparing a new Chaparral trailer.

"This was my favorite Funny Car," said Ivo. "At the Winternationals, I was running right up there with Prudhomme. But I kicked out the rods during the burnout up against him in the finals or I would have won the thing."

He also made the finals in Seattle and Oregon, which he credits to the fact that he was twisting the wrenches again. "The car was really running good, because I was working on it as crew chief and primary head wrench myself," he said. "I grabbed the reigns again because I didn't have a marriage or anything else to deal with at the time."

But the Arrow ate him alive with expenses. To save money Ivo backed off from running the Arrow as hard as he would have liked. He became an also-ran. He couldn't afford to be the killer driver he once was.

Ivo crashed the car hard in Epping, New Hampshire, and had to invest additional dollars to repair it again. For the first time, Ivo ended up losing money that year. "But my name wasn't tarnished; it had always been strong," he said. "I was like an old movie star—even if I wasn't in a blockbuster film at the moment, I was still someone that people wanted to see race.

"I was somewhat discouraged, but I was at a point where I didn't want to completely quit racing. I had seen these jet cars run, though. . . ."

Ivo's third Funny Car was his favorite. Plus he was back in charge, calling the shots and being his own crew chief. This was one of the last times the car ran; it had been painted with just flat-black racing stripes after the crash at Epping, New Hampshire. This nighttime flame shot is spectacular. *Tommy Ivo collection*

Ivo's third and final year had him in a Plymouth Arrow–bodied Funny Car. Since he no longer had an affiliation with Dodge, he felt the Arrow body was the slickest aerodynamically. Here the Arrow does a healthy wheelie while balancing on the left-rear wheel. *Tommy Ivo collection*

Ivo's last trip to New England Dragway in Epping, New Hampshire. At the conclusion of this run, he crashed heavily in the shutdown area when another racer plowed into the back of his car. The losses for the year were in excess of $40,000, convincing Ivo to call it quits. *Tommy Ivo collection*

Ivo's car (left) was slammed by Tim Kushi's *Yankee Sizzler* Funny Car when Kushi's accelerator stuck wide open at Epping, New Hampshire The two cars went off the track at high speed, somehow missing all the telephone poles. *Dave Milcarek photo*

Ivo and Kushi's cars after the crash. Both cars were rebuildable, but it would mean an operating loss on the year for Ivo. It was an expense Ivo could not afford. *Dave Milcarek photo*

Earlier in Ivo's career, he was offered a ride in Art Arfons' jet-powered
***Cyclops.* It was built for racing at the Bonneville Salt Flats, but he also**
ran it occasionally at drag strips. "The car had a passenger seat, so
I took a ride with him in the early seventies," said Ivo. "At the time,
dragsters were running at two hundred forty miles per hour, but Arfons'
jet car could run two hundred ninety!"

By 1980, Ivo didn't want to race the Funny Car anymore. "It was
taking major sponsorship funding and an army of crewmembers to run a
Funny Car properly," said Ivo. "The days of making a good living from
match racing were over, along with any free time on the road. The days of
having any fun on tour were gone."

Ivo decided to give up competitive drag racing and was determined
to become successful in an exhibition jet car. "People love these jets," he
said. "At idle I could hit the afterburner and put out a huge fireball."

Ron Attebury built the chassis and Ivo designed a swoopy, Can
Am–inspired body with an air dam. Jet cars were still in their infancy and
somewhat crude in design, comprised mostly of a jet engine and little or no
bodywork.

So with his new state-of-the-art jet car, which was hauled around the
country in a new glass-sided trailer, Ivo was once again the class act in a
new field.

He purchased his jet engines from a military junkyard in Arizona.
"You could buy one of these motors for twenty-five dollars," said Ivo.
"Not too bad for eight thousand horsepower. It was the most impressive
thing I had ever driven. But it was frightening when it was driven on these
little tracks that were no wider than a driveway."

The jet engine was a 900-pound compressor that ran at 15,000 rpm.
He rigged the parachute control onto the throttle so that the fuel would be
cut when he engaged the chute. If the engine was still running when the
parachute was deployed, the flame would have burned it up in the process
and there would be no way to stop with just the brakes.

"It would accelerate like a Super Stock car at the starting line," Ivo
recalled. "But instead of running from zero to one hundred in an instant
like the dragsters did, then begin slowing down the acceleration curve, the
jet would go from two hundred to three hundred in an instant as it started
packing even more air into the compressor. It was the most awesome thing
I ever drove."

Ron Attebury fits Ivo for his new jet dragster
chassis. Thankfully the design again put Ivo in
front of the engine. *Tommy Ivo collection*

Ivo installed two chutes on the car: an average size chute and a huge cargo-type emergency chute. His logic was that if you needed to use the big chute, you'd already be halfway through the shutdown area before you realized you needed it. Its stopping power was so great that the car's rear wheels would be lifted off the ground upon deployment.

Ivo once raced the car at Thompson, Ohio, where the drag strip is built on a rolling landscape. The track was built on level ground, but at the lights, the shutdown area went downhill at a six-degree grade. When his jet car reached the finish line, Ivo was in for quite an exciting ride. "I went out into the air because the compressor still hadn't slowed down, so it was still pushing," he said. "The thing came off the ground about eight feet. And there was a slight cross breeze blowing, which had me land right along the edge of the track.

Chicken-Shit Light

Art Arfons once offered Ivo a chance to ride shotgun in his jet-powered dragster. The passenger seat was way on the other side of the jet engine, so driver and passenger couldn't see each other. Arfons instructed Ivo that if he got scared, he should hit the button on the dashboard, which would let him know he should shut it down.

Little did Ivo know that the button was hooked up to a revolving police light on the top of the jet engine, which was known as the "Chicken-Shit Light."

Ivo sat to the right of the big motor and Arfons sat to the left. The "Chicken-Shit Light" is visible between the two men. *Tommy Ivo collection*

The announcer knew all about it and told all the fans in the grandstands during the run when Ivo couldn't hear it, that if the light went off, the passenger got too scared to ride it out to the finish line under power.

"Well, I wasn't about to hit that button for any reason anyway," said Ivo. "But if I had and was told what had gone on, I would have had to exit the car in the shutdown area, walk through the woods to the highway, and hitchhike back to the motel. I certainly couldn't have gone back into the pits again."

Ivo said that fans loved the balls of fire that spit out of the exhaust on jet dragsters *(above)*. On the return road at Orange County, Ivo's jet belches out a healthy flame. *Tommy Ivo collection*

Looking like a Formula 1 car built on the wrong side of the tracks *(left)*, Ivo used a Can-Am car as inspiration when styling the jet dragster's body. *Tommy Ivo collection*

"Wouldn't you know it, but it had rained the day before, so it was all mud. It stopped from three hundred miles per hour to zero in about four hundred feet. I about got sifted through the shoulder harness. My head got thrown so far forward that it crushed the front side of three vertebrae in the back of my neck. I think I came real close to pulling the spinal cord out of my skull, like what happened to Dale Earnhardt."

Because of his neck injury, at the next day's race in Englishtown, Ivo asked all his buddies if they wanted to drive the jet car, but he had no takers. The car didn't get hurt at all, so Ivo just drove it himself. He campaigned a jet car for the balance of the 1980 season, then sold it to a buyer in Seattle.

The cheapest horsepower on the planet! Ivo drove to Arizona and bought 8,000-horsepower surplus jet engines *(above)* from a J-34 Banshee Fighter Plane for $25 apiece. It was the most impressive car Ivo had ever driven. *Tommy Ivo collection*

The cockpit *(right)* of Ivo's jet dragster had no gas pedal—only a hand throttle. When the throttle was pulled backward, the jet accelerated; when it was pushed forward, it shut off the throttle and the chute came out. *Tommy Ivo collection*

The jet car accelerated from 200 to 300 in nothing flat *(opposite)*. Once, when it became slightly airborne and landed in mud, it decelerated almost as quickly, crushing three vertebrae in Ivo's neck. *Tommy Ivo collection*

Ivo's priorities were clearly changing. He built the jet Funny Car at the same time he was building a 3,000-square-foot addition to his home.

It was another one of Ivo's cars that never was. He built it, got it running, then immediately sold it off. "I got gun-shy," he said. "I had a guy build the car, but the chassis tubes were only welded on the top, not on the bottom. These things were running so fast and the mortality rate was really getting high. A bunch of guys had already died in jet cars."

Ivo called the new owner of his jet Funny Car and told him that he had a full-season tour for the car scheduled if he wanted to tour it across the country. He agreed, so Ivo promoted the car and accompanied it on the road, but didn't drive it. "I wanted to spend my spare time building my house," he said.

Ivo sold the jet Funny Car in 1981, but visited the new owner in 2002 and climbed back into the cockpit for this photo. The car has been restored. *Tommy Ivo collection*

Ivo only tested the jet Funny Car once, at San Fernando Drag Strip, but because he didn't care for the construction, he sold it. He went on tour with the new owner of the old jet dragster, but he never drove it. *Tommy Ivo collection*

It was 1982 and Ivo's 30th year in drag racing. He had put in many, many miles—one quarter mile at a time—since asking "What's the drags?" soon after purchasing his 1952 Buick at age 16.

He wanted to leave the racing industry with class, to make a proud goodbye to the fans, the competitors, and the promoters he had worked with for three decades. Then one day while he was working on his home, he drove a different route back from buying a load of bricks. He drove through an alley behind a string of stores and shops and saw something he hadn't seen in a long time. Behind a speed shop in Glendale, near his Burbank home, was the old trailer that used to haul his four-motor car.

He inquired about it and was told the race car was, in fact, still inside the trailer, where it had sat for at least a decade after blowing one of its motors.

He purchased the entire rig for $20,000.

"This would be my final tour," he said. "I was forty-six years old and would make one more lap of the country and visit the old tracks I've raced all these years.

"This was my signature car. Whenever you read about Tommy Ivo, you always read about or saw a photo of this car."

It sounded like a fairytale opportunity to bring down the curtain on a brilliant driving career.

Tom McCourry had purchased the *Showboat* from Ivo at the end of 1963. He campaigned the car as the *Showboat* for a couple of years before fitting it with the *WagonMaster* body to freshen up its fan appeal as Funny Cars were just becoming popular.

The Tom Hanna aluminum body resembled a Buick Roadmaster station wagon in miniature, hence its name. Ivo invested another $20,000 to restore the car, but decided to leave the attractive body on the chassis and campaign the car with Tommy Ivo graphics. He did all the work himself in the same two-car garage where he built the car 20 years earlier.

Ivo did what he did so well for so many years, contacting drag strip promoters around the United States to arrange his farewell tour. But on only his third stop, at a rural drag strip in Saskatoon, Saskatchewan, Ivo experienced a traumatic, life-changing event.

The track had been affected by winter frost heaves that caused slight undulations in the pavement. Ivo was running his car hard when

continued on page 214

For Ivo's last tour of the United States, he reunited with his old four-motor dragster and hoped to visit all the drag strips he had raced on for the past three decades. The Hanna-built body featured a Riviera-type front end and a luggage rack. *Tommy Ivo collection*

McCourry contracted with body fabricator Tom Hanna to build the *WagonMaster* body out of aluminum. Barris sued McCourry for taking his idea to a competitor. *Tommy Ivo collection*

The new body on the *Showboat (above)* was spectacular. The idea actually came from George Barris, but McCourry didn't want to pay the price Barris had quoted to do the job. *Tommy Ivo collection*

McCourry races the *WagonMaster* in Minnesota Dragways in Coon Rapids *(right)*. Even though it now had a body installed, the car still smoked all four tires, much to the delight of the fans. *Tommy Ivo collection*

Ivo's friend Tom McCourry purchased Ivo's *Showboat* four-motor dragster and campaigned it for a number of years with an aluminum body made to resemble a Buick station wagon. *Tommy Ivo collection*

In typical Ivo fashion, the *WagonMaster* was highly detailed. Because the Hanna body was so beautiful, he felt it couldn't be improved if he converted it back into a dragster. *Tommy Ivo collection*

it bottomed out on one of the slightly raised heaves. At slower speeds it would seem like a slight bump, but at high acceleration, it became severe.

He flew home to undergo tests. He didn't harm his spinal cord but crushed three vertebrae in his backbone just below the shoulder. Doctors said that he needed to wear a body brace but would be fine. Of course, the doctors reminded him that he couldn't drive a race car again. "I broke my back, and . . . was forced to retire forever," he said.

Ironically, Ivo, who had lived through a terrifying 240–mile–per–hour crash in 1974 without injury, was forced to retire after hitting a bump in

Ivo restored the *WagonMaster*, purchased a new truck and glass-sided trailer and hit the road one last time. *Tommy Ivo collection*

the road eight years later. This was tragic news for Ivo, who had hoped for one last speed-lap of North America. But, alas, it was not to be. His brilliant carrier was cut short not on his terms.

He hired another driver to fulfill his contracted race appearances, and he accompanied the car to the races to represent his "brand." His hired driver, Rick Johnson, made it easy for Ivo to say goodbye to racing.

"He thought he was my boss, my taskmaster," said Ivo. "He was such a prima donna, and he knew I needed him. He'd yell at me all the time. I didn't want anything to do with racing anymore after that."

Extravagant Trailers

A description of Tommy Ivo's vehicles wouldn't be complete without discussion of the haulers that transported them. When most of his contemporaries were still hauling their dragsters on crude open trailers, Ivo was decades ahead, with enclosed trailers of his own design.

Ivo built his own trailers in the driveway of his Burbank home. When he and a handful of fellow racers were invited to race in England in 1964, Ivo was the only racer who brought an enclosed trailer for his dragster. His car would be protected in the event that traditional British weather dampened the day. His trailer also had a sleeping compartment. When he was racing in the States, if he couldn't find a motel open during summer tourist season, he didn't have to sleep in the car, as he saw Garlits do on many occasions.

It was during the trip to England, though, that he actually got the idea for his future trailer design—a design that would further his fame. "I saw these modern buses in England that had huge, full-size windows on the side that ran from the passenger's elbow up into the roof," Ivo explained. "At the same time in the States, we had these crude old Greyhound buses with these little porthole windows. So I sat in one of those slick buses and realized that this was the ticket. I figured that if I built a trailer with glass sides, fans could look at my cars to their hearts' content. The idea took two years to become reality."

Ivo planned his new trailer concept while he was touring. When he got home, he knew exactly what he was going to do. "I ordered a bunch of four-inch-square tubing with quarter-inch wall thickness," he said. "I had it all drawn out. Rod Peppmuller would help me and would handle the welding. I'd tell him, 'Cut if off here, weld it there, make it sixteen feet here and put in an upright.'"

The windows in Ivo's trailers were not safety glass or Plexiglas. He used ¼-inch storefront glass because Plexiglas was too expensive and tended to scratch very easy. "We only broke one pane in all those years when a rear differential that I had carelessly placed in the car's glass compartment got loose and rolled into the glass," Ivo said.

Ivo decided to continue towing with his beloved Cadillacs even though the cars were grossly overburdened. "These two-door Caddies were tough cars," he said. "These cars were large and the trunks were so huge that you could have a party with ten people back there. But even though they weighed a hefty 4,000 pounds, a trailer with two dragsters and spare parts could easily weigh four times that much.

"Even though the trailers had electric brakes, the total rig was very underbraked. How we never crashed I'll never know, because we were always late and we were always speeding."

Ivo's first glass-sided trailer was inspired by the buses he had ridden in England two years earlier. Upon completion, though, it was involved in two accidents within 100 miles of leaving on national tour. *Tommy Ivo collection*

Ivo's first glass-sided trailer was found in a San Luis Obispo junkyard in 2007. The man offered it to Ivo for free, but Tommy had no idea what he would do with it. *Tommy Ivo collection*

This is the third trailer Ivo built. He no longer needed to haul two dragsters because his aluminum Hemi engine could be repaired easily. *Tommy Ivo collection*

Ivo preferred to travel at night because of his vampire sleeping cycles, but also because the roads were cooler, which was easier on the trailer tires. "Also there were less cops on the road," he said. "If we tried to cross the desert in the middle of the day we would blow tires off the thing. It was an adventure just getting from here to there."

Ivo remembered that with the multi-axle trailers, when a tire blew, he couldn't feel it when he was driving the tow car. He said he had to check the rearview mirrors continuously to see if smoke was billowing out. "One time when we were towing the streamliner dragster up to Fremont near San Francisco I looked in the mirror and saw smoke," he said. "I said, 'Darn, we blew a tire.' We got out and changed the tire and just threw the blown tire into the trailer and kept driving.

"A little while later, I looked in the mirror again and there was smoke again. 'This can't be,' I said, because I didn't have two spare tires. But when I got out and looked at the tires, they were all fine. It was then that I looked at the trailer and saw smoke coming out of it. When I opened the hatch, whoosh, the dragster was on fire! The blown tire that I had thrown in the back was still smoldering and had caught the dragster on fire.

"The cockpit canopy had already drooped from the heat, so we had to run it with a small windshield instead. Fortunately I hadn't painted the car yet."

John Force said Ivo's glass-sided haulers influenced him to build similar rigs decades later. "His trailers were state-of-the-art," said Force.

"Ivo could have unloaded his cars at appearances, but he was too cheap and it would have required more employees. So he'd just pull into a parking lot and sign autographs while fans looked into the trailer. When he drove down the road, people could see it was a race car. It's the same thing we're doing now, but we're just in a bigger arena."

Ivo's flashy tow cars often attracted as much attention as his dragsters. The front-wheel-drive Eldorado pulled a double-decker trailer that hauled two dragsters. *Tommy Ivo collection*

The Glass-Sided Truck and Corvette Push Car

Designer Steve
Swaja drew up this
sketch *(opposite
top)* of Ivo's
proposed Dodge-
truck hauler. It was
originally designed
as a single-axle
vehicle, but with
two dragsters and a
push car on the roof,
it was overweight
and handled poorly.
Ivo's Dodge hauler
(opposite bottom)
was a one-man car
show! The truck,
which was not
equipped with power
steering, hauled
two dragsters,
spare parts, and
the Corvette. It
also had a sleeping
compartment
behind the cab. A
second rear axle
was mounted when
state troopers
informed Ivo that the
vehicle was terribly
overweight. *Both
Tommy Ivo collection*

Sensing that they would get a fair amount of exposure during the 1969 drag racing season, Dodge gave Ivo a complimentary truck to haul his twin dragsters. Ivo fitted it out with a terrific glass-sided body and hauled his Corvette push car on the roof.

Unfortunately, the truck was a beast to drive and Ivo couldn't wait for the season to end.

"I listened to the truck salesman and did not order it with power steering," he said. "He convinced me that it would wander on the highway. The truck was almost impossible to steer around the pits.

"I also ordered it with only one rear axle on his advice, which was a mistake. At a weigh station in Louisiana during our first trip east, the troopers told us the rig was too heavy for just one rear axle. Fortunately, we were able to unload the Corvette from the roof and I drove it while Tarzan drove the truck. Before the troopers made us pull off the Corvette, I had been sleeping in the rear living quarters and could feel it sashaying down the road. We're lucky it didn't turn over, it was so unstable. We had a second axle welded in at the first industrial truck stop we found."

Ivo figures the entire rig, loaded with barrels of nitro, spare motors, tools, and the dragsters weighed at least 24,000 pounds.

"Tarzan was fearless in that truck," he said. "Once in Redding, Pennsylvania, we came to a bridge with a sign that read, 'Nothing Over 10,000 Pounds.' So I got out and walked across the bridge and then signaled Tarzan to come. He didn't care."

He made it.

The truck's small living quarters in the back were complete with refrigerator, stove, and sleeping area. "Tarzan would always complain that while he was driving, he could smell popcorn cooking in the back," said Ivo.

Driving the Corvette on and off the roof was Tarzan's job. Ivo said that it was like driving it off a cliff. "You couldn't see where you were going," he said. "It had to balance on these small ramps and it was a long way to the ground."

Whenever Ivo traveled near New York City, he liked to attend Broadway shows, so Tarzan would drive the 13-foot-5-inch-tall truck into the 13-foot-9-inch Lincoln Tunnel under the Hudson River to drop him off in the city. "I knew it would clear, but they had these little lights hanging down that just missed the roof of the Corvette," he said. "I got up there once and rode in the Corvette as Tarzan drove the truck. It didn't touch, but it was scary."

The season couldn't have ended too soon for Ivo and Tarzan. "We killed that truck in one year," said Ivo. "When we were through with it, I rented it to Bob Larivee, who promoted car shows back East. We parked it in front of Bob's house in Detroit and started to drive away. Then Tarzan

said, 'Wait, back up.' I thought he forgot something, so I backed up. He spit on the truck then said, 'OK, we can go.' He hated that truck."

The folks at Dodge were upset at Ivo when he revealed he intended to park a Corvette on the roof of their Dodge truck. "Dodge hated me," Ivo said. "When they saw a General Motors product on the roof, they just about had a heart attack. They wanted me to park a Dodge Dart or something like that on the roof."

Well, that was an old man's car and definitely not the "TV" Tommy image.

"My 'out' was I told them I needed a low car to make it under the thirteen-and-a-half -foot nationwide height requirement. Otherwise the roof of the Dart would have hit the first low bridge or tunnel and torn right off. But really, you couldn't push a dragster with a Dodge Dart!

"This is why I never got along with car companies, because I did what I wanted."

Ivo bought the Corvette used. He wanted a 454-powered car, but because of their popularity at the time, he couldn't find one, so he bought one with a 350-ci engine. It had an automatic, which was preferred over a manual gearbox when pushing a dragster. "We drove it back and forth to the hotel and to town," said Ivo. "I had it for just one year. It wasn't my personal car; I still had my Cadillac back home."

Once the Corvette push car came loose while riding on the roof of the truck. Ivo didn't tie down the car, but instead put it in park and engaged the emergency brake. When it came loose, Ivo and Tarzan felt the truck surging back and forth. "If it would have gone off the top, we would have been buying a new Corvette," said Ivo.

The Corvette push car traveled on the roof of the Dodge truck. Here Ivo shows the treacherous job of backing the car down from its 13-foot platform. The small-block car was purchased used in 1969. Ivo added the Keystone Classic wheels and a racing stripe. *Tommy Ivo collection*

Chapter Six

Leaving the Fast Lane Behind

Ivo crashed his Plymouth Arrow Funny Car hard in a race in Epping, New Hampshire. He was racing against Tim Kushi in the *Yankee Sizzler* Funny Car. Ivo beat Kushi at the start and as he approached the lights was about three car lengths ahead. Then all hell broke loose.

"Kushi's body pole broke and the right-hand side of the body of his car fell down onto the front wheel, which steered him right into my car as I was slowing down," said Ivo.

Simultaneously the body also jammed Kushi's accelerator wide open.

"So I just beat the guy handily and put out my chute and he steams into the back of my car full-tilt-boogie," said Ivo. "I'm thinking, 'What the heck was that?' thinking that most *BANG!*s come from the front, where the motor is. Then it goes *BANG!* again. I'm thinking maybe I just blew the rear end."

Both Ivo and Kushi were sliding through the shutdown area at high speed and completely out of control. They could have hit one of the many telephone poles or trees that lined the track, but luckily didn't. "I saved his life, because if he hadn't run into the back of me, he would have gone straight into the woods," said Ivo.

When his car came to a stop, through instinct Ivo jumped out and ran 50 feet from the car in case it was on fire. When he got a good distance away, he turned around to see what had caused the bang. It was only then that he realized Kushi had run into the back of his car.

Functionally, this was the end of Ivo's career. The cost of repairing the wreck plus all the appearances he missed cost him $40,000. "This was just another crippling blow to my finances," he said. "Forty grand in the seventies was a piece of change.

"It was just a bloody nightmare. If I had gone on, I would have needed a new eighteen-wheel transporter, a centrally located home base, a bunch of guys, and a huge sponsor. I was running the program out of my pocket and a bunch of smaller sponsors, and I was running out of money."

The sport of drag racing had changed significantly since Ivo first drag raced his 1952 Buick at 66.66 miles per hour. The sport that he helped build and nationalize was now passing him by.

Many of the drivers he had mentored were now finding sponsors and setting up professional racing organizations. Nearly all of those drivers

Because of his unusual skill set, Ivo was employed as stunt driver and technical specialist for the movie *Heart Like a Wheel* about Shirley Muldowney. *Tommy Ivo collection*

had totally left the match racing circuit behind and were instead racing for national points and winning championships. The tables had turned; now, because of the exposure television had brought to the NHRA, national events were where the big money was being made.

Drag racing had finally become what Ivo had always hoped it would be. But unfortunately, for once in his life, his timing was all wrong.

Adding to his declining competitiveness was the failure of his marriage to Inez, which was devastating to him.

Ivo could see his own personal shutdown area approaching.

Even though he would go on to race a couple of jet-powered cars, these were purely for fan entertainment. He would never again beat the likes of Don Prudhomme, Don Garlits, or Shirley Muldowney.

Ivo had always been a racer's racer—he built the cars, drove the truck, raced the car. He didn't fit into the template of the modern driver. Ivo felt more comfortable in a racing suit than a business suit; he'd rather hammer a piece of metal than hammer out a deal in a boardroom. He couldn't face a future where drivers only drove and crewmembers did all the work. For Ivo, it was about passion, not about business.

And he had become road-weary; he longed to sleep in his own bed every night and hang his clothes up in his own closet, not live out of a suitcase.

In 1982, at 46 years old, "TV" Tommy Ivo hung up his helmet forever.

Heart Like a Wheel

After he retired from driving the *WagonMaster* four-motor car because of a broken back, Muldowney asked Ivo to stunt drive her dragster for the biographical movie, *Heart Like a Wheel*.

"I had won the Top Fuel World Championship in 1980 and two weeks later I signed a contract for a movie," she said. "They insisted on the movie being authentic and wanted to use my actual car, so I rented them my championship car. Because of my racing schedule, I couldn't do the driving in the movie, so I recommended Mr. Hollywood himself, Tommy Ivo. He was the right size, he had the ability and knowledge of the sport."

Greg Sharp, curator at the NHRA museum, remembers the filming. "Ivo did this little ceremony at the World Finals where he burned his gloves on the starting line. To him, his racing days were over, and nobody was going to care who he was again."

The weight of Shirley's dragster almost doubled with the addition of all the camera equipment *(right)*, mounting hardware, and batteries. Ivo overinflated the tires so the cameras wouldn't shake on acceleration. *Tommy Ivo collection*

Ivo feels pretty good about the retirement deal he cut with the *Heart Like a Wheel* movie folks. He earned about $15,000 as technical consultant and stunt driver for the movie, which in 1982 was a good fee. "I was the only Munchkin who could fit in Shirley's car," said Ivo. "She was a petite little thing, barely over a hundred pounds, and I was just a little bit heavier. Plus I was camera-conscious, so I could advise them technically on camera placement."

But those cameras also made Ivo's driving job more difficult. Muldowney's Top Fuel car weighed about 1,500 pounds ready to race. But with all the cameras and equipment attached to the car, it weighed about

Ivo, wearing a brace to support his back, stands with Muldowney, racer/stunt driver Kelly Brown, and the director of photography during a break in the shooting. *Tommy Ivo collection*

twice that. Ivo had the tires overinflated to eliminate tire shake, which would have affected the onboard cameras.

Ivo had never driven a car as long as Muldowney's 280-inch chassis. "It was so comfortable, like a big spring," he said. "But even with that, my back hurt me so much that I could hardly get up each morning.

"I knew my driving career was definitely over at that point."

Life off the Road

"I had friends spread all over the United States," Ivo said. "I didn't have a friend base out here [in California] because I was working on the cars twenty-four/seven. Whether I was building a new car or trailer, booking appearances, lining up sponsors or whatever, it didn't leave a bunch of time for play when I was home."

But when Ivo traveled back East during his annual treks, his time for having fun was between racing weekends. "I had buddies in Chicago and everywhere," he said. "So when I quit racing, seeing friends around the country is what I missed the most. I mean, how could I fly to Boston to have lunch with someone?"

For the first time in his life, Ivo had nothing to do. This was an uncomfortable feeling for a guy who never stood in one place for very long. "I really didn't know what I was going to do once I realized I was retired from racing," he said. "Initially I just hung around the house."

Ivo tried a number of businesses—an auto repair shop, a moving and storage business—but after a high-speed life lived at more than 200 miles per hour, these alternate careers just didn't hold his interest very long.

"I was fifty-nine years old, which was exactly how old my father was when he died," said Ivo. "I decided I should retire completely before it was too late. Wouldn't you know it that today I'm seventy-four and doing great thanks to my mother's genes. All her siblings passed on well into their nineties."

Ivo's two interests were racing and travel, and now that he was retired from one, he had unlimited time to pursue the other. "It seems that every six months or so, my feet start itching and I need to go someplace," he said. "When I got married to Inez, we traveled on a honeymoon around the world, but it was only one day in Istanbul, one day in Tokyo, and so on. The idea was to see as much as possible in a short period of time. Now I had the time to really explore these countries."

There was also a new love interest in Ivo's life. Just as he had met Nancy Davidson, the girl across the street, at 13 years old, Ivo met Sandy Oomens, who lived down the street, at 52 years old.

"We both shared the same gypsy instincts for travel and the same lust for life," he said. "Once when we were in India, we had the option

Ivo met another girl from the neighborhood named Sandy Oomens who shared his love of travel. Ultimately she moved into Ivo's house and the two shared a happy 12 years.
Tommy Ivo collection

Oomens and Ivo traveled frequently and shared a love of adventure. Here they depart from a ship "somewhere in the world," said Ivo.
Tommy Ivo collection

of riding in a car or riding an elephant to the top of a mountain to see an ancient fortress. There was no question, we both decided to take the elephant at the same moment."

Eventually Sandy moved in with Ivo and the two started traveling the globe with some regularity. As Ivo says, it was adventure after adventure for years. "We were held up and robbed in Turkey with what appeared to be an antique pistol," he said. "We caught a cab in Egypt during a taxi strike and the strikers tried to turn us over. The driver, who was a scab, did a burnout and we got away, but we're lucky we didn't come home in body bags.

"Sandy and I took two trips per year and a number of more local trips, like to Las Vegas."

For Ivo's 60th birthday, he and Sandy purchased special airfare that allowed them to travel to as many places as they liked within one year as long as they went from east to west. They could also travel north and south as much as they desired, but they couldn't double back. "We got our money's worth from that package," he said.

A Life Well-Lived

Ivo fired up and drove the re-created *Barnstormer* at the Hot Rod Reunion's Cacklefest *(opposite)*. Ron Johnson built the clone in honor of Ivo's successful three-year campaign. *Paul Hutchins photo*

"When I look back at my career, I lived through it all," Ivo said. "One motor, two motors, four motors, sitting behind the motors, sitting in front of the motors, Funny Cars, jet cars—that's why I loved it so much; because it was like a giant R&D program all the time.

"Today it's what works, works. That's why everyone is running within a few hundredths of a second between each other. There's no experimentation anymore. Or at least on a scale compared to when I first started running anyway. It's just subtle innuendos here and there. To me, that wouldn't be any fun."

In 1991, when Ivo was 55 years old, he got a call from his lifelong rival, Don Garlits. Interestingly, there was nothing competitive about his phone call.

"We've finally worked out the plans for opening of the International Drag Racing Hall of Fame," Garlits told Ivo.

According to Garlits, a selection board, made up of Wally Parks (founder and chairman of the NHRA), Harry Hibler (publisher of *Hot Rod* magazine), Ted Jones (retired president of the IHRA), Dr. Robert C. Post (curator at large for the Smithsonian Institution), and Steve Evans (commentator for Diamond P Sports) had chosen Ivo as one of the founding members. He would be awarded this honor at the first annual gala awards banquet held in conjunction with the Gatornationals at Gainesville, Florida.

This was a shock to Ivo, who had gone into a nine-year, self-imposed exile, during which time he never even picked up a copy of *National Dragster*.

"When Tommy retired, he thought that was the end of drag racing for him," said Greg Sharp. "He didn't think after so many years that anyone would remember who he was. But at his 60th birthday in 1996, he drove his old four-motor car at a Goodguys

Where a drag strip once stood in Blaney, South Carolina, the town named the main street Ivo Circle in honor of Tommy Ivo. Here it intersects with a drive named after fellow drag racer Hubert Platt. *Tommy Ivo collection*

show in Indianapolis, and he had a hoot of a time. People stood in the rain for more than an hour to get his autograph. He thought to himself, 'Wow, they do remember who I am.'

"Now he's into a brand-new career; fifteen years into this nostalgia racing gig."

Ivo has had three of his cars—the twin-motor car, *Showboat*, and *Barnstormer*—replicated in high-end die-cast collectables by GMP, which has provided him great satisfaction.

"Until this nostalgia thing came around, nobody really cared about the older guys," said Don Prudhomme. "Suddenly, Ivo is everywhere again. I'm glad to see him get the credit he deserves. I'm not sentimental about Tommy Ivo, but it's nice to see that."

In 1992, Ivo was presented the first Lifetime Achievement Award by the NHRA at the first Hot Rod Reunion in Bakersfield.

In 1995, Ivo was named one of the 100 most influential people in racing by *Hot Rod* magazine. The one-time Las Vegas tribute also honored personalities like Andy Granatelli, Wally Parks, and Robert Petersen. Very few drag racers made the cut.

Car Craft magazine selected the All-Star Drag Racing Team, also in 1995. Ivo won the highest award of the evening, the "Ollie" Lifetime Achievement Award presented at a black-tie event at the Petersen Automotive Museum in Los Angeles.

The following year, he was awarded the first Justice Brothers Spotlight Award at the California Hot Rod Reunion in Bakersfield. It was named in his perpetual honor as the "Justice Brothers Tommy Ivo

Ivo received *Hot Rod* magazine's Lifetime Achievement Award in 1995 as one of the 100 most influential people in racing. *Tommy Ivo collection*

(Above left) Ivo jokes that Mario Andretti is one of the few people who he literally can look down upon. He met Andretti at the Motorsports Hall of Fame of America induction ceremony in 2005. *Jim Kelly photo (Above right)* "Being a hero has its advantages," said Ivo, who signs posters, T-shirts, and other items. *Tommy Ivo collection (Below)* Ivo and Linda Vaughn spend time together each year at the Hot Rod Reunion. *Tommy Ivo collection*

Spotlight Award" and is given annually to a person or group of people during the Bakersfield reunion.

One of the great honors of Ivo's life came when the Wally Parks NHRA Motorsports Museum installed a Tommy Ivo exhibit in 2002 that remained for two years. It took up half of the Hall of Champions it was so immense.

But the highlight of Ivo's career accolades came when he was inducted into the Motorsports Hall of Fame of America in 2005. The hall recognizes people from all forms of motorsports and Ivo was overwhelmed by the fact that he would now be able to call the likes of Dale Earnhardt, Mario Andretti, and Richard Petty his fellow hall of famers. "Big Daddy" Don Garlits himself was his inductor for the event.

The letter Ivo received to inform him he had been chosen read in part: "Voting was

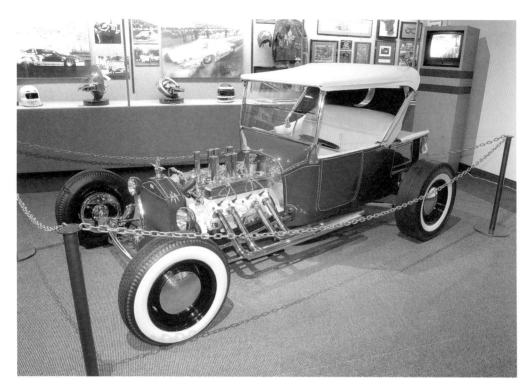

(Above) Ivo's incredible T-bucket hot rod was restored after being heavily modified by George Barris Kustoms. This is the car that Ivo wishes he still owned. *Robert Briggs photo (Below)* NHRA Motorsports Museum curator Greg Sharp (left) and museum director Steve Gibbs (right) posed with Ivo at the museum in 2002. *Tom West photo*

done by a select group of motorsport experts from across the nation. Because the Hall of Fame encompasses all forms of motorsports, and only one person is selected from each category, you are now a member of what is probably the most elite and distinguished group ever assembled in motorsports history."

Ivo joined other 2005 inductees Tom Sneva, Troy Ruttman, Benny Parsons, Hurley Haywood, John Holman and Ralph Moody, Jay Springsteen, and Danny Foster.

According to Ivo, being inducted into a drag racing hall of fame is a natural and someplace he would expect to eventually be nominated. But to be honored by the entire motorsport community—a very small portion of which have been drag racers—was a most special achievement for "TV" Tommy.

"That was a real feather in my cap," he said. "My bucket list is finally checked off."

Ivo gives his acceptance speech at Motorsports Hall of Fame of America induction. Ivo said that to be chosen by his peers for this award was better than winning an Oscar. *Tommy Ivo collection*

"TV" Tommy Ivo has led an amazing life, from an energetic kid missing his two front teeth to a man universally recognized as one of the greatest and most innovative drag racers of all time. Through hard work, creativity, and luck—combined with a touch of mischief—Ivo succeeded in the tough world of Hollywood and worked with some of the biggest stars in history. It was a life that most of us could only dream about.

Then at the peak of his career, he chucked it all to pursue his new love: drag racing.

But Ivo never did anything the easy way, and he never looked back. He could have easily ridden out his acting career through retirement. Not his style.

In racing, if he would have taken the easy way out, he wouldn't have gone through the trouble of engineering and building two-engine or four-engine dragsters, but instead would have built more conventional single-engine cars like his competitors were running. Again, not his style.

Ivo's unharnessed energy and love of adventure drove him far beyond his contemporaries. When the racing world turned right, Ivo turned left, charting his own path and writing his own rules. Whether he had earned top eliminator honors or found himself climbing out of a wrecked race car, Ivo rolled up his sleeves and went back to work, all without that famous Howdy Doody smile ever leaving his face.

It's what American heroes have always done. There is probably an important lesson there for all of us.

Acknowledgments

Thank you to Tommy Ivo, who endured days and days of my interviews. It was such a pleasure to sit face-to-face with one of my boyhood heroes and ask all the questions that every fan would ask if they had the same opportunity. Tommy rolled up his sleeves and read every word of this manuscript. Even after sitting at Tommy's dining-room table a dozen times over the course of a year, I had to admit to Tommy that I still couldn't believe I was sitting in front of the real "TV" Tommy Ivo.

Tommy goes to sleep in his California home when the sun comes up, and I get up on the East Coast very early in the morning, so we were almost in sync. Tommy's classic line to me near the end of his editing was, "See, we're both up at the same time, just at different ends of the day!"

Tommy, I took your edits seriously and I hope you are satisfied with the results.

Also, thanks to: Ed Janke, Joel Embick, Jim Miles, Bill Larzelere, Skip Torgerson, Bruce Meyer, Tom Jandt, Shirley Muldowney, George Calloway, John "Tarzan" Austin, Tom Madigan, Darlene Madigan, Tim Considine, Don Rackemann, Dave McClelland, John Coute, Ron Johnson, Tony Thacker, Kenny Safford, Greg Sharp, Don Prudhomme, Don Garlits, Tom McEwen, John Force, Art Chrisman, Skip Allum, Kent Fuller, Elon Werner, Orah Mae Millar, David Newhardt, Gary Schroeder, Dave Milcarek, Jim Miller and Steve Memishian at The American Hot Rod Foundation, and Gary McCourt.

And thanks to the team at Wolf Camera in Huntersville, North Carolina, who have helped me with photo processing on all my books!

Index